"Packed with practical, easy-to-digest advice, *7 Money Rules for Life* is a no-nonsense approach to money  ovides a road map to recovery driven by a real ⋯ life that isn't contingent on the actions of a⋯ ⋯t of life, take on the *7 Rules* and see what ha⋯

Rob Bernabé,
author, *Mind Your Own Mortgage*; speaker;
and former president of E*Trade Mortgage Corporation

"Without a doubt, Mary Hunt is in my 'Favorite Authors Hall of Fame.' Whether you are in desperate financial condition seeking hope and a plan or in good financial shape striving to be better, *7 Money Rules for Life* is a book I wish everyone would read and then pass on to their friends."

David Briggs,
director, Enrich Financial Ministry,
Central Christian Church of Arizona

"This powerful book is a must-read for you and everyone you care about. Mary Hunt provides a recipe for the art of living below your means. She is an advocate for ordinary people like you and me to do extraordinary things with our finances. *7 Money Rules for Life* comes loaded with tools that are applicable to all of us as we progress toward debt-proof living. Take control of your financial future!"

Stephen Komanapalli,
pastor, deputy chief of staff, Saddleback Church

"Simple rules of the road that cut through confusion, mystery, and misery. This is what Mary unfolds in her latest treasure that can transform the lives of individuals and families. Financial freedom is possible! And I'm sharing it with my kids, graduates, and newly marrieds. Top of my gift list for 2012!"

Lisa Rose,
founder, First Friday Women

"Mary gives us the raw reality of our deadly financial status but empowers us to overcome the obstacles by taking control of our own financial destiny. Every family should have this in their home."

Melissa Montana,
CEO/president, STAR Educational Media Network

"The brilliance of Mary Hunt's latest book, *7 Money Rules for Life*, is that it is a real story. She tells her story of how she got her family into massive consumer debt and their journey to financial health. *7 Money Rules for Life* inspires hope in seemingly hopeless situations and invites people to begin to take steps toward financial health. I can imagine people everywhere reading Mary's 7 *Money Rules* and saying, 'I can do that!'"

Allen Thiessen,
Stewardship Team Member,
Canadian Conference of Mennonite Brethren Churches

"This book can help no matter where you are financially. It is easy to read and easy to follow. If you put in a little effort, it will change your life! Well worth every penny!"

Marie Barger,
Debt-Proof-Living member and forum moderator

"Mary Hunt entered our life in 2006 and transformed it forever. With the help of Mary's rules, our commitment, and the grace of God, we were able to completely rid ourselves of credit card debt. We aren't completely debt-free yet but we are getting there day by day and step by step. We have a plan, and it works!"

Galen and Kathryn Gritts,
DPL members

"Mary has done it again! Rich, informative, enlightening, and educational. A simple read with a powerful message for anyone's financial life from Boomers to Gen X. Every household should have this book."

Kathleen Hairston,
DPL member and forum moderator

"Mary's 7 *Money Rules for Life* reads more like a conversation with a friend than a financial book, and comes from a place of understanding and encouragement. Those floundering in financial distress and wondering how they got there would find this book a great blueprint for how to climb out, create margin, and keep going."

Megan Lalli,
DPL member and community forums moderator

7

Money
Rules
for Life®

7

Money
Rules
for Life®

How to Take Control
of Your Financial Future

Mary Hunt

Revell

a division of Baker Publishing Group
Grand Rapids, Michigan

© 2012 by Mary Hunt

Published by Revell
a division of Baker Publishing Group
P.O. Box 6287, Grand Rapids, MI 49516-6287
www.revellbooks.com

Paperback edition published 2013
ISBN 978-0-8007-2253-1

Printed in the United States of America

The Library of Congress has cataloged the hardcover editon as follows:
Hunt, Mary, 1948–
    7 money rules for life : how to take control of your financial future / Mary Hunt.
        p.   cm.
    Includes bibliographical references and index.
    ISBN 978-0-8007-2112-1 (cloth)
    1. Finance, Personal. 2. Consumer credit. I. Title. II. Title: Seven money rules for life.
HG179.H8543 2012
332.024—dc23   5250 3249   1/14   2011033993

Scripture quotations are from the Holy Bible, New International Version®. NIV®. Copyright © 1973, 1978, 1984, 2011 by Biblica, Inc.™ Used by permission of Zondervan. All rights reserved worldwide. www.zondervan.com

Published in association with the literary agency of The Steve Laube Agency, 5025 N. Central Ave., #635, Phoenix, Arizona 85012-1502.

7 Money Rules for Life, Debt-Proof Living, Everyday Cheapskate, and Rapid Debt-Repayment Calculator are registered trademarks of Mary Hunt.

13 14 15 16 17 18 19   7 6 5 4 3 2 1

For Harold, again and always

Contents

Acknowledgments

I am fortunate to be surrounded by so many incredible friends and colleagues. Words cannot properly express the gratitude I have for them and for the profound impact they have had on my life and the writing of this book.

To Steve Laube, my agent, who works miracles on my behalf; to Cathy Hollenbeck, who shares my soul, knows my thoughts, and embodies the true meaning of loyalty and support. Thanks for embracing my mission and making it your own.

Thank you to Vicki Crumpton, editor extraordinaire, and the entire Revell and Baker Publishing Group team, especially Dwight Baker, Twila Bennett, and David Lewis. It's so good to be home.

Thank you to the many friends who keep me focused, on track, and happy: Susan Anderson, Marsha Willsey, Carol Vaughn, Herta Thiessen, Kathleen Chapman, Jan Sandberg, Mary Brock, Rosalie Copeland, Posy Lough, Kathy Chapman, Carolyn Walthall Haber, Melissa Montana, Paula

Cowan, Judy Bergman, Lynn Fann, and Hannah Linden. Your unconditional friendship means the world to me.

Thank you to those I consider my spiritual mentors, all of whom have taught me so much about stewardship, personal finance, and right living: Mark Copeland, Rob Bernabé, Dave Briggs, Dick Townsend, Rick Warren, Greg Laurie, Chip Ingram, Randy Alcorn, and Sarah Young.

Thanks, Dan and Molly Rice, for the keys to your lake house and Lexus for two weeks to write in total seclusion. I didn't know how brave I was.

Finally, thanks to my wonderful husband Harold, to my children, Jeremy, Josh and daughter-in-law Wendy, and to my grandson Eli, with love; I am so proud of you.

Introduction

The Great Recession hit Americans like a bucket of cold water in the face. We awakened from a 35-year drunken credit orgy with a terrible hangover. Almost overnight the American dream became a national nightmare as millions found themselves unemployed and underwater, owing more than they earn.[1]

Here we are, several years later, and things aren't much better. Unemployment is still high, gas prices continue to soar, it appears that the real estate market is still losing ground, and the US dollar is heading into a downward spiral.

Kinda makes you want to pull the covers up over your head and go back to sleep, doesn't it? Actually, that might not be such a bad idea because there's absolutely nothing you can do about any of that, anyway. So, I've got a better idea: forget the national economy. Stop dwelling on what you can't change and focus on the economy you do control—your personal economy.

We pay a high price for our financial illiteracy in the US. I have statistics you may find shocking. Honestly, they don't surprise me. I get it. I understand how we can be academically educated and socially prosperous in this great country, but also financially ignorant. I was. I couldn't be bothered with the daily grind of personal finances, budgeting, and planning ahead. Why bother? I had so many better things to do. Besides, I had credit.

I banked on the fact that the US economy all but guaranteed an upward spiral of increasing prosperity, better-paying jobs, and appreciating home values. There would always be plenty of jobs, lots of credit, unending supplies of loans to pay for kids' educations. If we worked hard, bigger and better cars and homes would always be within reach.

And I got away with that kind of attitude for years. But our lifestyle was built on a house of cards that could teeter only so long before it came crashing down.

I came to the end of the line and had to face just how ignorant and illiterate I was about money, or lose everything. Learning and applying simple, sound principles of money management saved my life.

Things are a lot different in America now than they were even five years ago. I believe that even greater challenges lay ahead. But despite all of that, I have very good news for you. Starting where you are right now, you can take control of your finances. You have the power to control your financial destiny.

The 7 Money Rules in this book have the power to change your life. I know, because they changed mine. The 7 Rules are the foundation on which my organization, Debt-Proof Living, is built and where over the past 20 years, thousands of people have learned how to get out of debt and live below their means.

7 Money Rules for Life will empower you to take control of your personal economy by helping you fix your finances one step at a time, moving you out of debt and ultimately to financial freedom, regardless of the country's progress.

If you're ready, so am I. Let's get going . . .

1 The Cost of Financial Ignorance

All the perplexities, confusion and distresses in America arise not from defects in the constitution or confederation, nor from want of honor or virtue, as much from downright ignorance of the nature of coin, credit, and circulation.

—John Adams, second president of the United States

If you had to pass a test to prove you could handle money before you could get your next paycheck—the way you have to pass a test to prove you can drive a car—would you get paid? The sad truth is that millions of us wouldn't. When it comes to managing money, Americans young and old are flunking out.[1]

The results from surveys, polls, and tests that measure financial literacy are in, and the results are grim. Most people don't have a clue.[2]

Jumpstart Coalition, the nonprofit organization that promotes personal finance education, concluded from results of its latest survey that three-quarters of Americans are ill-equipped to make critical personal financial decisions.[3]

A survey of Americans[4] conducted by the Harvard Business School found strikingly low levels of financial knowledge. Two-thirds of respondents didn't know how credit cards work. Many people didn't know the terms of their mortgage or the interest rate they're paying. And, at a time when we're borrowing more than ever, most Americans couldn't explain compound interest.

Only a minority of respondents had any idea that borrowing at an interest rate of 20 percent, compounded annually, will lead to a doubling of debt in fewer than five years.

The subprime mortgage fiasco that sent the US economy into a tailspin is the poster child for the national cost of financial ignorance. Even though unscrupulous lenders and overleveraged investment bankers played a huge part in escalating the madness, consumers had a choice when it came to entering into those mortgages. Financial illiteracy fueled the madness. Four years after the bubble burst, estimates are that one in four homeowners are underwater, making it nearly impossible to refinance their homes or relocate to take another job. How far under? Another report shows 5.5 million US households are tied to mortgages that are at least 20 percent higher than the current home value.[5]

It is heartbreaking to think that so many Americans were lured into toxic mortgages and home equity loans, unaware that they were willingly agreeing to big balloon payments on interest-only contracts. Or found adjustable rates to be the pathway to smaller payments that allowed them to buy more expensive homes. The sad truth that I am hearing now from so many people is that they didn't have even the foggiest idea what the lender was talking about, and assumed everything would be okay.

Not surprisingly, a study by the Federal Reserve Bank of Atlanta found that borrowers with the lowest math skills were four times more likely to have bought homes that wound up in foreclosure.[6]

The fallout from this rampant financial ignorance is shocking:

- 77 percent of Americans are living paycheck to paycheck with no savings or emergency preparedness, up from 49 percent in 2008.[7]

- Outstanding revolving credit card debt has reached $828 billion.[8]

- The average credit card debt per household with credit cards: $14,788 at 16.82 interest.[9]

- Credit card fees paid by low-knowledge individuals are 50 percent higher than those paid by an average cardholder.[10]

- Student loan debt in the US recently shot up to $850 billion and now exceeds the total credit card debt.[11]

- A shocking 43 percent of Americans have less than $10,000 saved for retirement, while 49 percent could cover less than one month's expenses if they lost their incomes.[12]

What grade would you give yourself? Knowing what you do know about money and managing your finances, how would you rate your financial proficiency, knowledge, and confidence to manage your massive lifetime income?

Massive? Yes, you read that right. In your lifetime, you will handle *millions* of dollars in earned income, and that's not a typo. Let me prove it to you.

Let's use the latest US Census median household income figure of $52,029.[13] Now multiply by 45, which is the commonly accepted number of income-producing years. Are you ready? The answer is $2,341,305. And that's an average. Your number could be significantly more.

I know what you're thinking, so let me address that. I realize that you may not have made $52,029 (insert your figure here) every year. But your income will not remain the same for the rest of your income-producing life, either. Over time, your income will increase. So consider it a kind of average, and a very conservative estimate at that.

My point is that when you look at the big picture, the total amount of money that will flow through your hands and which you will control during your lifetime is significant. You are a millionaire, receiving that fortune one paycheck at a time.

Managing your income skillfully is at least as important as your ability to drive a car. You worked hard to learn how to drive. You took a written test to prove you knew the laws and rules of your state. You took a road test to prove that you are a safe, knowledgeable driver.

Yet, chances are high that you entered adult life without any kind of financial training that would prepare you for handling something of such value and importance as a lifetime of income. And you didn't even get an operating manual.

If you did arrive at adulthood with a good grasp of personal finance and money management as a life skill, you are fortunate. That puts you miles ahead of many of your peers as you look forward to your income-producing future. Sadly, most people enter adulthood lacking personal financial intelligence. They have no rules to follow, not even a list of suggestions or any kind of mental framework for how to manage an income or even what that would look like.

Every day my email inbox bears witness to the high cost of financial ignorance. I hear from men and women who are overwhelmed by debt, have no savings, don't invest for retirement, go back to school on student loans because they're broke and can't get a job, find divorce to be a solution, and just flat-out make terrible financial decisions. And my mail is also peppered with cries for help.

"I'm just not good with money."

"I'll never have enough."

"I don't know where to start."

"I'm such a loser, I've made so many mistakes."

"My financial situation makes me so depressed."

"I'm so overwhelmed I am paralyzed."

"Just tell me what to do. I don't need to know why, just what and how!"

Can you identify? It is scary to be in a situation where the lifestyle you've chosen requires every last nickel of the income you produce just to get by. And that's in a good month. When something comes up that you didn't expect, it can throw your life into the kind of turmoil that has debt written all over it.

I know personally what a lack of financial training will do to you, and the ways financial ignorance can change the course of your life. Let me tell you my story . . .

2 My Story

Even when I'd get the ugly call from the bank, I never thought of myself as being overdrawn, I was just under-deposited!

—Mary Hunt

My pulse raced as I signed my name. What if the salesclerk called the bank to see if I had money in my account? Or worse, what if she called the police? I was about to attempt to pass a hot check, something I'd never done before, and I was sweating bullets.

Just days before, I'd arrived in Southern California and moved into the college dormitory, which would become my home for the next four years. The student handbook was filled with rules for student life and helpful hints, including information on how to open a student checking account in a local bank, which I did.

Fitting in and getting up to speed socially was a top priority, so when my roommate invited me to go to the mall, I jumped at the chance. Honestly, I'd never seen such an amazing place.

I have no idea what I bought that day, it was all so spur of the moment. The others girls were shopping, and I wanted to be cool and independent like them. Making my own decisions and getting to decide what I liked was new for me, and boy, did it feel good.

I experienced a few moments of anxiety as I traced in my mind what I was about to do. I knew that I didn't have enough money in the bank to buy anything. The good girl in me was cautiously reluctant. The naughty girl said, just go for it. Nothing's going to happen, and besides, you deserve what you want.

And so I wrote a check, knowing I didn't have the money in my account. This was back in the late sixties before the days of electronic checks, high-speed computers, and instantaneous transactions. I would soon get a paycheck from my new campus job, and with any luck I'd get it to the bank before this one cleared, and all would be well.

This powerful event, in some sick, twisted way, fulfilled the promise I made to myself at the ripe age of eleven: when I grow up, I am going to be rich.

The second of four children, I grew up in a sheltered environment. Looking back now, I can see that we were a frugal family, but at the time I didn't see it that way. My childhood perception was that we were dirt poor and poverty stricken. My mother didn't work, my father was a pastor, and I had to wear clothes from the thrift store. It was embarrassing. I hated my life and dreamed about how things would change when I grew up and could make my own decisions and have things other people had.

The Sears catalog was my planning tool. I'd secretly "shop" and make lists of all the beautiful linens, furniture, and household items I would buy to furnish my dream house. I found my future family in their respective sections of the catalog and outfitted all of us with beautiful new clothes. I "bought" my children toys and my husband a riding lawn mower. I even bought a white picket fence. I lived in a fantasy world, creating the life I would have one day when I was old enough to leave home.

Now, seven years later and far from home in a big, beautiful department store with checkbook in hand, I felt as if I'd arrived. I could buy anything I wanted. I felt rich, and it felt fantastic.

My experience that day was a defining moment that would change the course of my life. Simply knowing that as long as I could get away with it, I could have what I wanted even if I didn't have enough money to pay for it, changed me in ways that would all but ruin my life. We're not even talking about credit cards here. I managed to squeeze that kind of promise from a checking account.

It's not like I had experience with deceit or breaking rules. In fact, I'd always been a compliant, obedient child and certainly never one to flirt with dishonesty or anything else that might be considered sinful. In all of my strict upbringing, which mostly centered on what not to do, I didn't learn a thing about managing money. Reconciling a checking account was completely foreign to me. APY? A budget? Not a clue.

To this day I do not know if my parents assumed I would learn money management skills through some kind of financial osmosis. They may have thought that one semester of high school bookkeeping would set me on the right fiscal path.

Maybe they figured I'd do what many women did in those days, marry a man who would take care of all of the money details for me.

Most likely it didn't cross their minds to teach me how to handle the currency of life. It was simply not a topic that anyone talked about.

I did graduate from college and managed to stay out of jail in the process. Unfortunately, my financial shenanigans didn't stop with my first hot check that day at the mall.

I came to enjoy the option of being able to spend my money before I had it in my possession. I discovered that having more than one checking account allowed me to do that more efficiently because I could buy more time. Honestly, I didn't know that having checking accounts in several different banks and then passing checks between them in order to create more time to cover checks I'd written, a practice known as "check kiting,"[1] was illegal. I thought I'd discovered a very clever way to manage all the money I didn't have yet. I don't claim to have been a master of manipulation. I was pretty good at it, but now and then I'd mess up and get nasty phone calls from the bank or, on occasion, a merchant letting me know that my check had bounced. I hated when that happened.

Shortly after my twenty-second birthday, I made a big life decision I knew would fix my money problems and move me closer to my goal of being rich.

I got married. And I don't mean that I just got married. *I got married to a banker*. I was madly in love, of course, but it didn't hurt one bit to know I was marrying well.

It was shocking to me to learn after we'd been married for a few months that as a management trainee, Harold did not make the insane amounts of money I'd always associated with the banking profession. And it took even less time for that banker to discover that his new wife had, shall we say, a little problem with spending.

To say that I was a prime target for the consumer credit industry is putting it mildly. In my heart, I knew that a checking account was never intended to be a financing tool. It took a lot of effort to make that work. But a credit card? Now that was something completely different, and exactly the instrument I needed to kick up my buy-now-pay-later financial habit more than a few notches.

Companies were falling all over themselves to give me credit cards because, of course, they discovered that I was so creditworthy. (This was before the law was amended to make it illegal for companies to send out their credit cards unsolicited.) Even better, they trusted me with a lot of money (read: credit), which elevated my opinion of myself. After all, if they thought I could handle thousands of dollars in available credit, apparently I could. And wasn't that a pleasant surprise?

I began collecting credit cards the way some people collect baseball cards. It was fascinating to see just how many I could get. I didn't intend to use them, but I loved the sense of security I had just knowing they were safe in my wallet.

It didn't take long, however, for me to find plenty of reasons to use them. After all, I had emergencies. And since the reason for having the cards in the first place was to be prepared in case of emergency, I found it perfectly reasonable to use them in that way.

My *modus operandi* was simple: spend money until you run out, then spend credit to cover the rest. Or, use your credit to preserve your money. My method for handling money on any given day depended on how I was feeling at the moment. I would often default to the "if it feels good, do it" method, which was closely related to "if it's on sale, it's a sign that God wants me to buy it."

The arrivals of our two sons, Jeremy and Joshua, gave me new reasons to need more money, which meant chasing ever-increasing amounts of credit. What began as monthly balances that we could pay in full soon turned into only the minimum payments required each month. The debt grew little by little at first. It didn't seem like a big deal because the monthly payments seemed affordable.

It took no time at all for the line between Harold's income and our available credit to blur to the point that I lived as though credit was the same as income. Just one big pile of money with which to make the best life possible for my family. And when the pile would evaporate, I'd find more credit.

I learned quickly the various stores' and banks' credit card rules: use them often, pay the minimum monthly payment, and view credit limits as if they are gold stars on your character and personal worth. And if you need us to increase your credit limit? Just call!

Being a good consumer and playing by retailers' rules was like getting regular raises. While I didn't dwell on it, somewhere in the back of my mind I knew the debt I was amassing would have to be repaid. Someday. In another time and place, far, far away. I believed that it would all work out. Like magic.

When we'd been married for about 12 years, I begged Harold to quit the bank so we could start our own business and become rich entrepreneurs. I knew that his banker's salary would never cut it. Finally he did leave his job because he wanted to make me happy, and we became the newest independent distributors with a group that promised us that we would become rich.

We committed the two fatal errors of self-employment: we got into a business we knew nothing about and we did it with borrowed funds. Within four months my dream turned into our collective nightmare as we lost our business and walked away with nothing but more debt.

I didn't intend to ruin my life. But gradually, over time, I came this close to doing it. I made a horrible mess, one that put our home into threat of foreclosure and left us unemployed.

In the fall of 1982 my world came crashing down. I had no idea how much debt we had, but I knew it was a lot. There were even accounts and debts that Harold didn't know about. And that day, I found myself flat on the floor on my face. I've never felt so alone and afraid in my life. I had no more options, nowhere to turn, and no idea what to do. I was completely out of hope. That day was my turning point. Lying there on the floor, I knew that my only option was to look up, and that's when I had an amazing encounter with the God of the universe. For the first time I saw the ugliness of my greed, and what it had done to my life was almost more than I could bear. I wept in remorse for what I'd done. It wasn't my rotten luck, my husband's underpaying career, or any of the things I blamed that landed me in this pathetic place. It was me. I'd been demanding, self-serving, manipulative, and deceitful. I was in the worst jam imaginable, and I had taken my family with me. I had no idea what to do, except to call out to God and ask him to forgive me. I asked for another chance and an opportunity to pay back the debt and change my ways.

As I got up off the floor that day, the fog didn't lift to reveal a pile of money that would fix everything. But I knew

I'd been forgiven, and in that promise I found new hope that my life could be better.

You might assume that I, with my newly found determination to become money wise, together with my husband and his banking and finance background, would know exactly how to take charge of our personal finances. But you'd be wrong. Honestly, we didn't have a clue what to do.

Within a few weeks, through what I can see now as an amazing set of circumstances, I went to work as a part-time industrial property manager. Odd because I didn't seek that job, it came looking for me via a phone call out of the blue. A gentleman whom I'd met years before sought me out, offering me a job on terms that I could choose, to work in his family's real estate development company. For the next two years Harold and I reversed roles as I became the breadwinner and he a stay-at-home dad.

As I began receiving regular paychecks, I realized how ignorant I was about what to do with the money. Admitting that I didn't know it all was somehow refreshing. My heart had become tenderized, and that diluted my arrogance and pride, making me willing and eager to learn.

Compared to our bills and outstanding debts, a single paycheck was like a raindrop in the ocean. I mean, what's $400 when you're staring at one month's stack of past-due bills that added up to more than $4,000? It was beyond overwhelming.

Normally, my approach for how to spend such a piddly amount compared to the amount we needed to get current would have been something along the lines: "Since we don't have enough to pay all of the bills, let's buy groceries and then take the kids to Disneyland." But I'd just had a transformational experience. Even though I didn't know what to do with our personal finances, I knew that what I had been doing wasn't working. There had to be a change, and it needed to start now.

That's when I sat down and made a list. Little did I know that those first few written decisions for how we would appropriate any amount of money that came into our household would develop into the 7 Rules.

Over the years, as Harold and I walked through the dark night of debt and into the bright light of solvency and then on to founding Debt-Proof Living, I've reworked, refined, expanded, and consolidated the rules to the 7 I'll share with you in this book. Since making that turn on the road to financial devastation, more than a few people have expressed their shock by asking, "How could you let that happen?" My answer is simple. At several defining moments in my life (the day I stood in that department store with my new checkbook in hand; the day I accepted a credit card without telling my husband; the day I filled out the form to get my own secret post office box where I could receive statements for my secret credit cards, to name a few), I faced critical decision points, and each time I made the wrong choice.

I have no doubt that at the time I made them I could have convincingly defended those choices, but that would not have made them the right decisions. Absent a simple set of rules to follow for how to manage money well, I had no foundation on which to stand; no fundamentals to turn to.

I learned a lot from my journey back from the brink. I didn't become an heiress or win the lottery. I worked harder than I'd ever worked in my life. The process shaped my attitudes and beliefs. As God provided the opportunities, we paid back more than $100,000 in unsecured debt. Now I find the greatest joy in my life's work of leading others out of debt.

Through it all, the most important thing I've learned is this: money management is not difficult. Personal finance is not brain surgery. Anyone can learn how to apply a simple set of reliably sound rules to manage money and discover the path to financial freedom.

While I have determined that I will not live with regret, I do wonder how things might have turned out if someone had taught me simple principles for making financial decisions. I believe that I would have saved years of heartache and untold amounts of money to say nothing of lost opportunities. At those pivotal defining moments I would have made a different decision because a specific Rule would have been my guide. I would have known, almost instinctively, what to do, not come up with some wild, manipulative response in the absence of a specific guiding principle on which to rely.

I am so grateful for how God has taken the broken pieces of my life and woven them into a tapestry of beauty that reflects his grace and mercy. It is a daily testament to the way that God can take even our worst mistakes and turn them into something of value.

If your current financial situation has you all tied up in knots and stressed out of your mind, get ready for some relief. Things are not likely to change overnight, but perhaps for the first time you will know what to do to get the change started.

Wouldn't it be nice to find out that there are simple rules of the road that can cut through all of the confusion, mystery, and misery and enable us to get our financial lives on track? I have great news . . . there are.

3 Financial Intelligence Will Improve Your Life

The rewards for "getting it" have never been so immense, and the penalties for financial ignorance have never been so stiff.

—Niall Ferguson

Money mastery is not hard. It's the lies we believe about what money can do for us and the dumb decisions we make out of ignorance that cause so much misery. Once the misery sets in, then personal finance and money management can take on high levels of difficulty, to the point we are overwhelmed.

I hate to think what life would be like if there were no rules. From morning to night, every day of our lives, we live by some kind of rules.

Most families have rules of the house—expectations of conduct and decorum that are expected of all those residing therein, with age-appropriate consequences for failure to follow the rules.

If you've ever built or remodeled a home, you know something about rules in local building codes, which I will admit that to a layperson can appear to be a total waste of time and money. Still, those rules make for much better, safer, and more pleasant living conditions when all is said and done.

Like guideposts that mark the sides of the road, rules keep us from wandering off into danger. They offer assurance that we're on the right path.

Meet the 7 Rules

Over the years, I have taken the lessons I've learned, the mistakes I've made, the principles in Scripture, and wisdom from experts, counselors, and teachers whom I respect and boiled it all down to these simple rules that changed my life.

Rule 1: Spend Less Than You Earn

Rule 2: Save for the Future

Rule 3: Give Some Away

Rule 4: Anticipate Your Irregular Expenses

Rule 5: Tell Your Money Where to Go

Rule 6: Manage Your Credit

Rule 7: Borrow Only What You Know You Can Repay

The 7 Rules are not seasonal, nor are they based on emotion. They work for people who have lots of money as well as those who are struggling to survive on a single income or are between jobs.

The 7 Rules are for every income, every age, every stage of life. They apply to an unemployment check, an allowance, a paycheck, a dividend check, a bonus check, a trust account, an inheritance, and even a vast estate.

The 7 Rules apply to individuals and families who are deeply in debt, just as they do for those who are debt free. The rules do not change, because they are based on timeless truth and unchanging principles. They're like anchors that keep us from drifting off course or running aground even in the midst of a storm when visibility is all but lost.

Here's the best part: the 7 Rules are simple. So simple, in fact, they can fit on the back of a business card. Given 15 minutes you could even memorize them. In fact, I recommend you do.

Why You Should Care

About once a month or so I travel to speak to groups of people about money, something I love to do. Just before I step to the podium, I look out at the audience. I can almost hear what they're thinking: *Great, she's going to talk about money. Why should we care?* That question revs my engine and puts me into my zone. I hope you're asking the same question, right now. Here are four reasons:

1. Because money is important. Its impact is also emotional, spiritual, and personal, which can be tricky, especially the emotional part.
2. Because money impacts our lives. It determines where we live, what we drive, where the kids go to school. It's the means by which we pay our bills, protect our families, and prepare for the future. Wrong choices and bad decisions can turn an otherwise pleasant life into a miserable existence.

3. Because Americans are finding themselves more financially challenged as prices soar but paychecks remain stagnant. Recovery from the Great Recession is turning out to be slow and uncertain. Those sitting on the sidelines waiting to move ahead with their lives until everything gets back to "normal" may be in for a very long and disappointing season.

4. Because you may be called upon to handle a significant amount of money in the future. It might be an inheritance, a job promotion, or a sizable investment portfolio. Or it might be simply a second chance for getting things right. Will you be ready?

Clean Sweep

I'm a sucker for home improvement TV shows, especially the ones that focus on organization and de-cluttering. That's where I learned this important tip on organization: don't try to organize your clutter. Instead, move everything out to create a clean, clear, open space. Then go through everything you removed, sorting and evaluating what you want to keep. Next, bring things back into the room in an orderly manner.

In your mind's eye, picture your financial life as a big room that is filled with every aspect of your current financial situation: bills, debts, income, taxes, mortgage, savings, student loans, unemployment, retirement concerns—everything that you identify as part of your money life.

Using the "clean sweep" approach, empty that room. Haul everything out onto the lawn or somewhere far from your mind's view. Don't stop to ponder over stuff, just round it up and move it out.

Mentally, give that space a good "cleaning" or whatever it takes for you to be able to take a deep breath, sit back, and enjoy the absence of financial noise.

It is against the backdrop of this fresh, clean slate that I want to offer you the 7 simple money rules in theory so you can grasp how they work and fit together, without interference from what may be going on with your finances at the moment.

We are going to do this one chapter, one rule at a time. I will explain the rule then tell you why the rule is integral to your life. I will include clear instructions, suggestions, and frequently asked questions for how to apply the rules to your life starting with your current financial situation. Think of this as an orderly way to move items back into the "cleaned room" of your personal finances. I can't promise an overnight transformation. But by facing the truth and applying the rules, change can begin right away.

4 Rule 1

Spend Less Than You Earn

Contentment is a pearl of great price, and whoever procures it at the expense of ten thousand desires makes a wise and happy choice.

—John Balguy, eighteenth-century theologian

The first rule is so simple, I hope it doesn't prompt you to blurt out, "Come on, Mary, everyone knows *that*." I promised you that this is not difficult. This first money rule for life is so logical but so misunderstood, many people miss it. There's a lot of competition for your mind and your wallet these days and a big world out there that would rather you not pay too much attention to the first rule.

Rule 1: Spend less than you earn.

Of all 7 Rules, this one takes top honors. It is the most important not because the others are less important, but because until you spend less than you earn, you can forget the other six.

Without Rule 1 it will be impossible to master the rest. Curiously, the other six make it possible for you to follow Rule 1. In fact, the 7 Rules are so dependent on one another they have a symbiotic relationship.

Truthfully, I would be surprised if this is the first time you have heard of the concept that you should spend less than you earn. It's possible to confuse it with a similar concept: don't spend money you don't have. I agree that they sound much alike, but there is a big difference between "spend less" and "don't spend more."

The 77 percent of US households that are admittedly living paycheck to paycheck could claim that they are not spending more money than they have. However, they're spending every nickel they do have, then they white-knuckle it until the next paycheck, barely hanging on from one paycheck or other source of income to the next.

What a dangerous and stressful way to live. Granted, theoretically the paycheck-to-paycheck style of money management does not necessarily mean living on credit or spending more than one's income. But in practice it does. But I digress. Back to Rule 1.

Margin is another word for freedom. Spending less than you earn is the way to create margin. Margin is good because it allows you to breathe, to think and relax. Margin is another name for profit or reserves.

Spending less than you earn is the only way you will experience financial freedom. Contrary to how it might sound to you at first, Rule 1 isn't about restriction. It's about freedom—freedom from want, freedom from fear of running out of money, freedom from reliance on credit, freedom from being under the economic thumb of others.

My grandparents knew a thing or two about Rule 1. They would have never dreamed of spending all that Grandpa earned at his job as an insurance salesman, because how else could they make sure they had their nest egg funded at a level where they could sleep at night? They also had Grandma's rainy day fund, a source of mystery and delight for her grandchildren. She spoke of it with respect and reverence in a way that was warm and endearing.

They had no outside sources on which to rely if they ran a little short or if Grandpa had a slow month. They created their own safety net rather than relying on Visa or MasterCard to bail them out of every little emergency.

Living beyond your means, the ultimate violation of Rule 1, is a horrible way to live because the resulting debt and self-indulgent mind-set leads to depression and anxiety. And that opens the door to all kinds of heartache.

At my organization, Debt-Proof Living, bringing dignity to the art of living below your means is included in our statement of purpose. Living in a way that you spend less than you earn is a safe, dignified, and God-honoring way to live.

No matter how we say it—spend less than you earn, earn more than you spend, live below your means—my goal is that by the time you finish this chapter you will experience a great awakening for why consistently spending less than you earn is the key to experiencing freedom from debt.

It's About Attitude

Rule 1 is less about money and more about the most fundamental asset that you have in life: your attitude. Attitude is the way you respond to everything in life. Your beliefs and feelings shape your attitude. Your attitude is the only thing in your life over which you have complete control. Read that last sentence again.

Sure, you have influence over a number of people in your life, but absolute control? No. Your ability to make decisions gives you some control in other areas, but nothing other than your attitude—your thoughts and actions—is completely in your control.

Before you can make the decision to take control of your money, you must be convinced and committed. Spending less than you earn isn't something that happens to you. It is something you make happen. It is a decision. It's the attitude you choose for how you will conduct your life and manage your money.

Tattoo this on your brain: *attitude is everything*. Write it on the inside of your eyelids so it's the first thing you see every morning and the last thing at night.

For some, it is a challenging change, a new way of life that requires learning, devotion, and tenacity. Making a serious commitment to spending less than you earn will be the first giant step you take toward finding financial freedom.

A Look at Income and Expenses

Years ago when I fell on my face before God in abject humility and remorse for how I'd spent my family into oblivion, I saw for the first time that my spending was the problem. It was out of control. The resulting debt was threatening my marriage, home, and family. Spending more money than we earned—even if it was just a little bit more—had a horrific cumulative effect.

I knew that I spent too much money and used too much credit. But I didn't really get the full impact of how a single shopping spree had a wide-reaching effect on my life until I came face-to-face with simple visual illustrations like those that follow. Seeing this illustrated almost knocked me out. How could I have been so foolish, so ignorant and lacking discernment?

I want to show you visually what affected me so profoundly and helped me to understand the long-term effect of overspending.

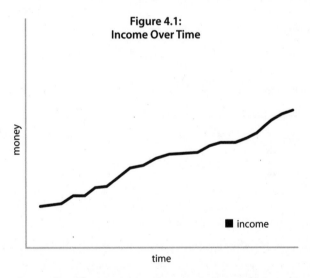

**Figure 4.1:
Income Over Time**

Let's say this chart represents your income from when you got your first job to now. Or allow it to represent your household income from the time you married and established your home. This is not scientific but rather intended to represent the money flow into your life.

When you got your first job, you started out at a low rate of pay, then gradually it increased either because you changed jobs or got promotions and pay increases with the same employer. The details are not important, only that you see that over the course of years, typically, one's income increases.

Now let's add spending to the picture.

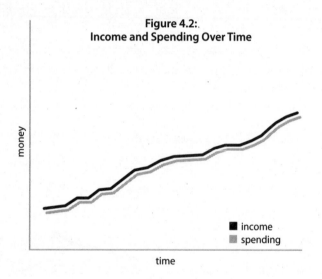

Figure 4.2:.
Income and Spending Over Time

This is an illustration of a household that spends what it earns. Technically, this is a picture of "living within your means." Spending matches income, precarious as that might be. The lines should really be one on top of the other to indicate that for this family or individual, it's money in and money out, in equal amounts. But that would be difficult for you to see on this two-dimensional page, so I've moved the lines apart ever so slightly.

This is also what it looks like to live from paycheck to paycheck, on a really good month. Whatever is in the paycheck is the amount of money available to spend until the next paycheck. Of course it's not as easy as this illustration might suggest, because show me whose real-life expenses track identically to one's pay. But in theory this illustration is perfect for showing the paycheck-to-paycheck lifestyle. Income determines spending.

In this scenario, when the breadwinner gets a raise, as indicated by the upward climb of the income line, expenses increase at the same rate because there's more money to spend. There's no margin for the unexpected, no savings, just a passive decision to hang on until next payday, week after week, month after month.

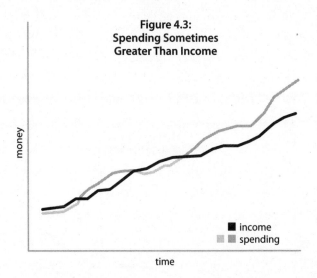

Figure 4.3:
Spending Sometimes
Greater Than Income

money

■ income
■ spending

time

This graphic depicts the household that can't quite manage to live paycheck to paycheck. When the month turns out to last longer than the money, these folks resort to credit to bridge the gap. Debt comes and goes, which you can see as these folks pay off the debt, and for a season they are committed to spending less than their income. That's fairly impressive until we see how long that lasted.

Things get out of control once again as perhaps a child goes off to college or gets married, or they bought a new home and their expenses increased significantly more than their income could cover. It could be due to a season of unemployment for which they were not prepared or, most likely, the ugly accumulation of revolving debt.

Consistent overspending fueled by credit can quickly create a situation like the one you see in figure 4.3. Here, these people are destined to head into their retirement years spinning their wheels because their debt controls them. Without a major change of heart, mind, and behavior they have little hope of bringing that spending line down prior to the income line dropping severely as their paycheck becomes a Social Security check.

Before you get too depressed, let's look at an income and spending scenario guided by Rule 1: spend less than you earn.

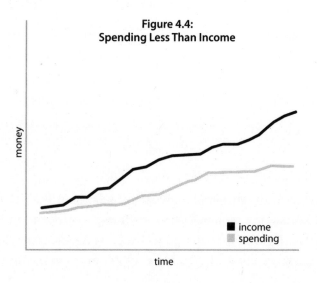

Figure 4.4:
Spending Less Than Income

money

time

■ income
■ spending

Here we see the same income line as in the previous example. But, look at the spending. In the beginning it tracks income pretty closely but as income increases, spending does not increase to match. The space or "gap" between the two lines indicates money this family or individual does not spend because they keep their spending less than income. That space represents the money that allows them to save, give, and invest.

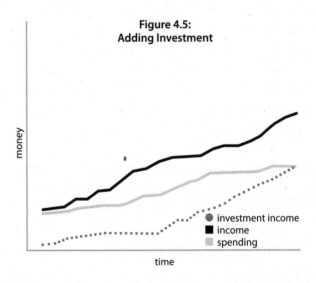

Figure 4.5:
Adding Investment

In this graphic we see the same income and spending with an added line accounting for the money they are saving and investing to grow for the future. This could be through an employer-sponsored 401(k) plan and/or individual investing. At any rate of return, the investment income remains very low, often appearing to be nonexistent for quite a while.

Over time, as the growth or "return on investment" begins to "compound" (a term that means the growth becomes principal and then that amount begins to earn interest or experience growth as well), notice how the "investment income" line begins to ascend.

Lowering spending to increase investment income is the way to grow wealth. It is the way that people with ordinary incomes are able to do extraordinary things. The combination of time and living consistently below your means is a formula that works for anyone regardless of income level.

Take another look at the investment income line, specifically where it takes a noticeable turn upward until it meets the spending line. Although it may take time, eventually investment income will equal spending. This is a critical point, because this is the point at which you begin to experience financial freedom. Your investments are creating enough income to cover your expenses, making you less and less dependent on your job as your source of income, even though you may choose to continue to work so that your investments can grow undisturbed.

This couldn't happen if that spending line was exactly the same as the income line throughout all of the income-producing years. Or, if spending was routinely greater than income.

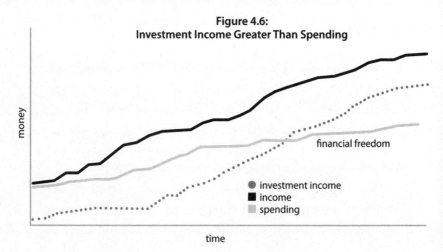

Figure 4.6:
Investment Income Greater Than Spending

money

financial freedom

● investment income
■ income
▪ spending

time

This is a longer view of the previous graphic, showing that even after reaching financial freedom, spending remains low so that investment income can continue to grow. In this scenario, because you continue to work, you are not making withdrawals from your investments to cover living expenses.

The way to get from where you are now to where you are spending less than you earn is to assess every way you spend your income. By doing so, you will find that place of contentment where you are not constantly striving to have more, because you have chosen to be satisfied with less.

You become financially free when your passive income (the income that your investments earn as opposed to the income you receive from working) exceeds your expenses.

Needs vs. Wants

Our basic needs as humans are few: shelter, food, and clothing. Everything else, with the possible exception of taxes and medical attention, is a "want." But in reality, distinguishing a need from a want is not quite that easy. Living in a country where there is so much abundance and so many choices, a sense of entitlement can muddy the waters when it comes to what we want and what we need.

Because our resources are finite, we have to make decisions about which wants to fulfill. The strong pull of the culture can skew our thinking, making us believe that we don't have a choice. That so many things are must-haves. We're persuaded to think we have to spend money in certain ways and amounts. In reality, our spending on wants is a choice. The only ones who "need" us to spend on wants are the marketers!

So, if you're managing a big monthly payment on a fancy car, that car has morphed from a want into a need, but only because you chose to buy it on credit and selected that particular payment schedule.

It's easy to confuse needs with wants. You work hard, so you deserve to drive a nice car, right? Whether it's a time-share on Maui (everyone needs a vacation) or a phone upgrade (you definitely need a smart phone), magazine-cover-worthy Christmas celebrations, or just a few meals out each week— your sense of entitlement can cloud your thinking when it comes to what you want and what you really need.

Thankfully, we live in a society where items beyond the bare-bones fundamentals of food and shelter can be considered "needs." Your personal liberty will help you to make those kinds of determinations. What may be a "need" in my life could show up under "want" for you.

Ugly Attitudes of Entitlement

Most people, I believe, have an elevated sense of entitlement simply because they have no idea how fortunate they are. Face it: if you've never been hungry, never wondered where you would sleep, and never had to go without shoes, your thinking may be skewed about minimum creature comforts.

If every winter your family took a ski vacation; if every Christmas you were delighted to find your entire wish list wrapped and piled under the tree; if every summer you went to camp; if you started every school year with new clothes, shoes, and the best school supplies; if you had your own cell phone and car before you were old enough to vote (and

Daddy's gas card just in case), why would you think you were entitled to any less as an adult?

Compare the houses our parents and grandparents were raised in to those we're living in now.

In 1950, the average new single-family home in the US was 983 square feet.[1] It was normal for a family to have one bathroom and for two or three growing children to share a bedroom. By 1970, the average home grew to 1,695 square feet with two bathrooms. By 2008, that average home had expanded to 2,629 square feet with multiple bathrooms, and the addition of a family room was considered standard fare.[2]

There was a time when only the rich and famous could afford granite counters and marble floors. Now for many those are essential, plus a bedroom for every child, a living room, family room, Wii-sized media room,[3] walk-in pantry, his and hers showers, a home office, and kids' playroom.

While it's easy to criticize the younger generation for its rampant sense of entitlement, it's not just a problem of youth and immaturity. Even our vocabulary now includes words to describe this sense of entitlement that crosses all demographics, words like "consumerism" and "shopaholic," "affluenza," "entitlitus," "conspicuous consumption," "retail therapy," and "consumercide." We don't need definitions. We know what these terms mean, which is some version of, "I work hard for my money; I deserve to have _____ (insert your luxury item of choice)."

Great. But then you have to keep working even harder to pay for the things you deserve to have because you work so hard. What's the point of spending money we don't have on a want, and then working so hard to pay for it that we never enjoy the item we thought would bring pleasure?

The Stuff of Entitlement

The rapidly growing self-storage industry in the US and Canada bears testimony to the fact that we have become so addicted to stuff and a materialistic way of life, with serious difficulty distinguishing between needs and wants. More than 10.8 million US households are paying a public storage facility, every month, to store the stuff they deserve and just could not live without.

At last count, there were just shy of 51,000 storage facilities—more than seven times the number of Starbucks in the US.[4] Within those storage facilities there are approximately 17.5 million individual storage units, covering 2.3 billion square feet. One out of every ten US households now rents a unit in which to cram a whole lot of stuff they never use.

This Seductive Culture

Advertising has become such a big part of our culture, we are mostly unaware of the ways it influences our desires, the ways we spend our money, and to what extent we're willing to legally obligate money we haven't earned yet. Simply put, advertising is the art of convincing people to spend money they do or do not have for something they do not need.

Advertisers rely on marketing theory that says people are driven by four things: fear, guilt, greed, and the need for approval. Ads are designed to throw us off balance emotionally to create discontent.

First, the commercial advertisement grabs our attention then proceeds to stir up one or more of the emotions I just mentioned, followed by a product and a promise to alleviate the discomfort it created in the first place.

Several years ago, I read in the *New York Times* that the average American adult is the target of some 5,000 commercial ads in a single day.[5] How outrageous is that? Sure, we live in a highly commercialized society, but 5,000 ads? In a single day? I figured that had to be an exaggeration.

One day I decided to conduct my own test. I would count the ads I heard or saw in my typical day. I knew it couldn't come anywhere close to thousands, but I needed to find out for sure.

The next morning the radio alarm sounded, and before I could open my eyes, I put two hash marks on my score pad. So prolific were the ads on television, I could barely keep an accurate count and get ready at the same time.

Of course, I had to count every message, banner, business placard, real estate sign, billboard, license plate frame, bumper sticker, commercial vehicle, and bus I saw on the way to work, all the while being careful not to miss any radio ads. Good thing I wasn't driving.

Reading the newspaper boosted my count significantly as did flipping through a few magazines. Have you ever counted the ads in a typical woman's magazine? Try it sometime.

Logging onto the internet shot my count through the roof. The mail arrived at 10:00 a.m., and that's when I surrendered. Not only was it impossible to get anything done while counting the commercial influences on my fairly low-key, ho-hum kind of a day, I couldn't keep up with the pace. It was a mind-boggling exercise.

So, 5,000 ads per adult per day? Easy! And after only a few hours of intense focus I became keenly aware of the way that advertising creates desire and dissatisfaction in me to the point that I began to "need" things and services I didn't know existed only hours before.

My experiment gave me a fresh awareness of the strong pull of the culture and the way advertising manipulates our feelings. Honestly, it was a little scary to realize just how vulnerable we are to the stealthy persuaders around us. It's like advertisers are forever sneaking up on us, just waiting for that moment when they can catch us unaware and entice us to hand over our money in ways we hadn't even dreamed.

What can we do? We can try to remember to switch the channel or toss the latest cool mail order catalog into the recycling bin without looking, but honestly, how long will we keep that up?

What we need is not change but rather transformation. We need to stop hoping that someday, somehow if we work hard enough we'll make enough money to have all the things that will finally make us happy. We need to stop believing that it's okay to have things we want now, even if we cannot afford to pay for them.

Taking responsibility for the choices you make, identifying most of them as wants, not true needs, can be frightening. But when you see that you do have choices, you'll stop feeling like a victim of your circumstances and realize that you really do have the power to control the choices you make with your money.

Here's the Secret

What follows may be the single most important thing you will read in this book, so I hope you are paying attention:

choosing contentment as a way of life is the only way to win the battle between needs vs. wants. Contentment is choosing to be happy with what you have, while not always desiring something more. Contentment is not something we achieve, it is a choice we make. It is an attitude we learn. It's a decision we make to buy what we need and want what we have.

Prosperity does not bring contentment, and poverty cannot take it away. Read that again. If prosperity were the secret for contentment, Hollywood, the NBA, and the National Lottery Winners Association (I made the last one up) would be the happiest places on earth.

Contentment is that settled place where we are at peace knowing that while we may not have it all, we do have enough. Enough for survival, enough for comfort, and enough to meet our needs.

Confronting yourself is a great way to build your strength against the strong current of commercialization. True needs are never discovered while standing in the aisle at Target. If you *needed* bright orange cookware, an iPad, or whatever thing you're about to pop into your shopping cart, you knew that before you arrived. It would have been on your list, physically or at least mentally.

The best way I know to separate needs from wants is through self-assessment. Here's what I mean.

Before making a spending decision, ask yourself these kinds of questions and expect honest answers.

- Do I need this? This is a personal thing. There is no universal list of appropriate "needs."
- Do I have something already that will do just as well? You have no idea how many times I have to stop right

here once I'm honest with myself and remember that I do have three other black cardigan sweaters, or whatever thing that might be tempting me at the moment.

- Am I sure this is a good value? I've learned the hard way that just because something is on sale doesn't mean it's a good value. It might be a bogus sale, meaning that the price is still higher than the competition. Or that lawn mower might be really cheap but of such poor quality, it will only last one season, which makes it really expensive and a lousy value.

- Do I have the cash to pay for it? I'm sure we could both agree that there are things we need but we just cannot afford. If you cannot afford to pay for it but must put it on credit instead, that should stop you in your tracks and send you to the next question.

- Could I delay the purchase for a few weeks or months? Just because you need something doesn't mean that you need it now. Delaying the purchase will give you time to save the money to pay for it without using credit.

- Am I willing to delay my decision for 24 hours before acting? A cooling-off period gives you time to rethink your decision.

This flowchart is a much-refined version of something I wrote down and attached to the front of my wallet many years ago. I realized I needed something to interrupt my impulsive nature.

In a moment of strength, I made myself a promise that I would run through these yes and no questions before I bought anything of value, which I determined back then to be $20 or more.

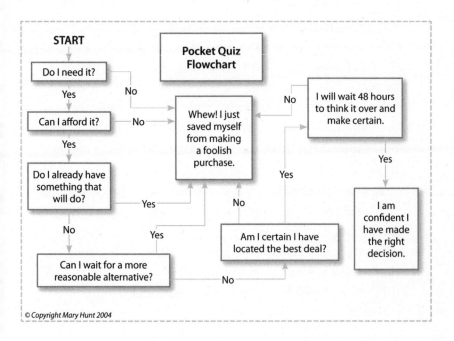

Here's what you are going to discover using my pocket flowchart: it's like a pause button that lets you take a breath and focus on what you're about to do. It offers you time to think and regroup. And if you get to the very end and still believe this is a purchase you must make, don't be surprised if after your self-imposed 24-hour waiting period, you change your mind.

I cannot tell you how many times I've gotten all the way to the cooling-off period, gone home, and then never purchased the item. It's like once I get out of the vicinity of whatever it was that I believed I truly needed, the desire dissipated, which is quite amusing considering how many times I've convinced myself that it really was something I needed.

Widen the Gap

Creating more space between what you earn and what you spend is the way to build wealth, reduce stress, create options, and find peace of mind. Living below your means is an honorable way to conduct your life. It is the money you don't spend that gives you the freedom to live the life you love and the life God has for you.

It would be remarkable if you could change just one thing that would result in an overnight widening of the gap between the income and spending lines on your personal Time and Money chart. Realistically, that's not going to happen. But don't despair. Changes you make today will begin to make a difference, even if it's only a small amount at a time.

12 Easy Ways

Since 1992, when I founded Debt-Proof Living, I've been on a mission to help people discover ways to widen the gap between their income and expenses. In response, readers have sent in their favorite tips to share with me and my DPL family. While I can't share all ten thousand (more by the time you read this), here for your enjoyment are a dozen good ones.

1. Borrow and share. Stop buying things you are so sure you need like yard tools or DVDs. If you won't need to use it more than occasionally, borrowing or renting makes sense.

2. Avoid the mall. There are some who see a shopping mall as an entertainment destination. Wandering around to see what's new is called browsing, a financially deadly pastime.

If you truly need something, shop sales at discount stores for that specific item and then leave.

3. Limit exposure to advertisements. Commercials and print ads, as previously mentioned, are designed to make you feel incomplete, out of style, and unfulfilled. When you cannot avoid, analyze. Verbalize the inadequacy the ad is attempting to convey, then rebut it.

4. Live with cash. For your day-to-day spending, lock up the plastic. Use cash only. Prepare to be amazed as you wake up from your comatose spending. Statistics bear out this fact: you spend more when you pay with plastic. Even if it's a plastic debit card. Retailers much prefer that you shop with plastic because you will routinely spend 30 percent more, simply because you don't have to be as careful as you are when you have only a limited amount of cash. Use this fact and embrace the inconvenience of cash to reduce your spending. It is so worth the effort.

5. Spend-free day. Designate one day per week that you will not spend anything at all except for life's absolute essentials. Nothing. Gear up, plan ahead, and then stick to it. When it becomes comfortable, make it two days a week. Expect your brain to wake up in ways you had not anticipated. I know some who have taken this all the way to a spend-free month, once each year.

6. Save the difference. When you switch to a cheaper phone service, find the perfect shoes on sale, use coupons at the supermarket—actually save your "savings" in a bank account. Unless you deposit the difference between what you spent and what you would have spent had that item not been on sale, you haven't really "saved" anything.

7. Stay healthy. Medical problems can drain bank accounts in a big hurry, even when you have insurance. Anything you

can do to improve your health will go a long way to widening the gap.

8. Cook in. As food prices climb, eating out is getting so expensive! By the time you add tax and tip, eating out can be one huge budget buster. Save it for the occasional special occasion and start eating at home. All seven days of the week. If you don't know how to cook, learn. Coffee lover? Make it at home. A $3.95 coffee five days a week is $1,027 in a year.

9. Pare down. If your home is typical, you are overrun with stuff, much of which you don't need, don't use, and don't even want. Determine that not only will you stop adding to your stuff, you'll make a commitment to liquidate. Turn that stuff into cash. There are myriad websites where you can get cash for used books, DVDs, video games. Become an eBay seller, a Craigslist expert, and a Freecycler.

10. Don't pay retail. You may have to wait for something to go on sale. That's good, because more likely than not, you'll change your mind or even forget about it in the interim.

11. Unfriend the Joneses. Admit it. You've been trying to keep up with them, haven't you? Now it's time to let them go because this is not a competition. It's your life, your future. It'll be a lot easier if you can convince yourself that they're buried in debt trying to impress you.

12. Increase income. Cutting expenses will eventually have its limitation. There comes a time when you need to do anything you can to bring in extra money, even if you already work a full-time job. Consider overtime at work, dog walking, babysitting, tutoring, or using any skill that's unique to you for which others will pay you to do that work for them: web designing, party planning, teaching music lessons are only a few ideas.

Never underestimate even the smallest effort to spend less or earn more. It all adds up, and faster than you might think.

Quick-Start Recovery

If the income and spending lines on your personal Time and Money graph have switched places—your spending often exceeds your income—we will not assume that you've been robbing banks to pull off such a feat. It doesn't mean that you've done anything illegal. Sadly, overspending becomes an acceptable way of life for some people.

We live in a world of easy credit that's readily available and takes many forms: home equity lines of credit, 401(k) account raids, credit card accounts, overdraft protection, payday loans, and for some, the ever-reliable Bank of Mom and Dad.

You may be part of the 77 percent paycheck-to-paycheck crowd (page 19). You're not necessarily spending over your income every month but you squeak by, scrounging to find loose change under the sofa cushions to buy milk and diapers as you wait breathlessly for your next paycheck. And you're sick of it.

How can you possibly begin to spend less than you earn when you have not found success trying to live on 100 percent of your paycheck? You're so far underwater, you're reaching for scuba gear.

Look, I am not going to sugarcoat the truth: you are in a dangerous position. You do not have the luxury to ease your way out. You need to make radical, dramatic, life-saving changes.

1. Stop spending. Just stop. If it is not required to preserve life (examples: basic food, gasoline to get to work, medication, rent) do not buy a thing. Round up all of your plastic and put it away in a safe place that is not easily accessible.

2. Finish reading this book. We're only on Rule 1, there is more to come. As I told you, Rule 1 lays the foundation for those that follow. I will not leave you hanging.

3. Downsize your lifestyle. I would not be surprised to learn that you have cut your expenses to the bone, and that you can cut no further. I respect your efforts, but if you are unable to live on less than you earn, you have a lot more cutting to go. It's called austerity, and that surpasses frugality. Austerity may require that you move to a cheaper neighborhood or move in with family. Sell your extra cars in favor of public transportation. I don't know exactly what you need to do, but somewhere between the bare necessities of life and where you are now is a place where you are spending less than you earn.

4. Pray. As we move through the rules, you are going to learn that I am a person of faith. I believe that we are here by God's design as stewards of all of the good things he has for our enjoyment. Talk to God about your situation. While I don't know what you are going through, he does. He loves you and cares about your life. God will wait patiently until you come to the end of yourself and surrender your life and your will to his loving care.

5 Rule 2

Save for the Future

> A part of all you earn is yours to keep. It should be not less than a tenth no matter how little you earn.
>
> —George S. Clason

If you've ever felt as though some kind of invisible force is conspiring against you to make sure you never get ahead, you may be more right than you think.

You have two enemies with a single purpose: to destroy your contentment and make it difficult, if not impossible, to spend less than you earn. Their names are Fear and Greed. They're liars and thieves and will go to amazing lengths to undermine and sabotage your efforts to take control of your money.

In this chapter we take on our enemy Fear, that will do all it can to make sure that you never find contentment. This enemy will stalk you and keep you in its grip using worry, anxiety, and frustration to beat you down.

Fear makes you worry about everything from running out of money to getting fired. Fear scoffs and insists that you'll never get out of debt, that you'll have to work until you're 85, and even then you'll probably outlive your money and end up living under a bridge.

Financial fear leads to stress, depression, insomnia, and worse. It can mess with your mind and lead you to think irrational thoughts.

Fear is a strong enemy but quite a weakling compared to the power you have to defeat it.

It's time to knock the life out of this first enemy, Fear.

Rule 2: As you receive income, transfer 10 percent of it into long-term savings.

I love Rule 2 for its simplicity and power to disarm fear and worry. The most straightforward of all 7 Rules, Rule 2 is almost a no-brainer. Simple math and a dogged determination are all that is required.

I understand that if you are one who really wrestles with money fears, this might sound too easy. It is simple, you're right about that, and it works.

Rule 2 might also sound scary if you're already struggling to live on 100 percent of your income. How can I expect you to keep up but on 10 percent less? Don't worry. There's plenty of credible data out there to suggest that if you are not taking good care of your money, at least 10 percent of your income is leaking away undetected. Good management can plug the leaks to recover the money required to apply Rule 2 to your life.

The Antidote for Fear

The antidote for financial fear is money in the bank. It changes everything because you lose that broke feeling.

Money in the bank changes your outlook because it changes your attitude. A nice stash of cash, tucked away in a high-yield savings or money market account returns big doses of peace of mind.

(You may have just chuckled at my use of the words "high yield" referring to savings accounts these days when interest rates are so low as to be almost nonexistent. It is a relative term that refers to a category of savings vehicles that do pay a higher rate of interest than what you'll find at a typical bank or credit union.)

Money in the bank creates margin. Margin helps you to think more clearly and to make decisions that are not driven by fear. As your savings grow, so do your options. And with options come hope for the future.

I have come to the conclusion that people are fearful in direct proportion to how prepared they are to go through a season of financial hardship. Those who have no money in the bank and just enough food in the house to get through the week feel as though they're sitting on a time bomb.

They're terrified and worried sick because instead of saving money, they're racking up debt, which just makes things all the more terrifying. They're just barely hanging on from one paycheck to the next. If I could share with them some of the mail I've received recently from ordinary people who have suddenly found themselves unemployed after following Rule 2 for many years, I'm quite sure I'd have their attention.

One family told me how they added up their savings and realized they had enough money to live exactly as they had been living for at least six months. If they made some sacrifices, they could last for a year without tapping any retirement funds.

The feeling of freedom they described was amazing. Knowing they were prepared financially, they could more easily deal with the emotions and challenges of losing the family income. They viewed it as an adventure, not a catastrophe.

In this particular family, the father, who was the sole breadwinner, didn't feel an enormous pressure to jump at the first job offer he could find. Because they were so well prepared for this upheaval, he had the option to hold out for a job he wanted rather than one he might have had to tolerate just to get back to work. He did find a new job after just three months, and amazingly because the family pulled together and cut out all unnecessary spending, they didn't even touch their savings. But knowing it was there if needed, they related how they were more willing to make big sacrifices just to see how long they could survive on the breadwinner's unemployment check.

Self-Reliance

Saving money strategically and with purpose does more than accumulate money in a safe place. It develops character traits of self-reliance and financial maturity. And patience.

There was a time when people had no choice but to prepare for their own emergencies. They had no safety net, also known as a credit card, to cover them when things went wrong.

The world changed in 1950 when Frank McNamara invented the first multi-use credit card, Diners Club Charge Card. Seven years later at the age of 40, McNamara died having seen his invention expand to nearly one half million Diners Club cardholders. I'm sure that even McNamara would be shocked if he knew where his idea has gone 50-plus years since he checked out.

The credit card changed the world in terms of self-reliance and the advancement of personal entitlement. But more than that, it blinded us to what should be instinctual—the need to save for the future as a matter of survival.

We've come to accept credit cards as the way to deal with emergencies. That's how I lobbied to get my first credit card. I needed it, just in case of an emergency. I wouldn't be surprised at all if that's the reason you got one as well. Most people have bought into the marketing hype that the way to prepare for financial emergencies is to have plenty of credit available.

Survival Instinct

All of creation has been designed with the will to survive. That is especially fascinating to study in the animal world. Who hasn't seen squirrels and ants storing up during seasons of bounty in preparation for lean times ahead?

We humans are endowed with survival instincts, not unlike animals but with at least one distinction: we can think and reason. And ironically that, it seems, has become our downfall when it comes to keeping our financial survival skills intact.

Relying on credit cards to cover us in emergencies may seem like a quick solution to the problem. But it only feeds fear and worry, because instead of lightening the financial load, it increases it, opening the door to more fear and worry.

What Went Wrong?

I place a great deal of blame on the consumer credit industry, which has managed to brainwash an entire society into believing that saving money is not a priority.

The message of consumer credit is, "Go ahead, spend what you have, get all you deserve. Don't worry about anything! We'll be right here to help out if you experience some kind of emergency. You need our credit card so you will be prepared for emergencies. You work hard, there are so many things in life to be enjoyed, so go ahead and live it up!" Granted, I'm no ad writer, but you get my point.

Don't get me wrong. I am not saying that no one saves money. In fact, I wouldn't be at all surprised if you have some kind of retirement account somewhere that you think of as a savings account (it's not). And maybe a jar or two of coins, a stack of US savings bonds your grandparents stuck in a shoe box, or even a savings account plus some CDs at your bank or credit union. Good. Really, I applaud your efforts. But that doesn't mean, necessarily, that Rule 2 is alive and operating well in your life.

Saving for the future needs to find its way back to your natural instinct as a responsible human being. You cannot continue to spend all that you earn (Rule 1). You must save systematically for the future as if your life depends on it (good, you recognized Rule 2). It just might.

Rule 2 in Action

When you receive money from any source, before you think about spending it, transfer 10 percent into your long-term savings account—no questions, no excuses, and no exceptions. Don't think, just do it. Anyone can put money aside, at any level of income. You just have to do it. Saving money is simple. In no time this action will become a habit that you repeat so often it becomes automatic.

Rule 2 is not fulfilled with contributions into your retirement account, like a 401(k). This 10 percent comes off the top of your take-home pay—the money in your possession over which you have control.

Let me stop a moment to define a few terms. When I speak of Rule 2 savings as "long term," this distinguishes these funds from money you may be saving to buy a new sofa or for your family's summer vacation. That would be more short-term savings and a matter we see in Rule 4 to come.

Your Rule 2 long-term savings should be seen as insurance against big, serious emergencies that may be in your future: losing your income, an expensive medical event, or some other surprise emergency expense that hits hard.

Retirement accounts, such as a 401(k), 403(b), IRA, and types of "tax advantaged" accounts (meaning that you are saving pre-tax dollars) are not savings accounts because the money is out of your reach now and until you are 59 1/2. These accounts hold your retirement income—money you will need much later. Resorting to getting your hands on the funds ahead of time would be very costly to you, and a downright terrible idea. You do not want to think of tax-advantaged accounts as your source of income during times of unemployment or some other way to deal with a financial emergency. That is the role for your "long term" savings, which you can think of as your emergency fund (or your Contingency Fund, if you are part of Debt-Proof Living).

Make It Easy

The purpose of Rule 2 is to create a lifelong habit of saving for the long term, starting with an emergency fund.

Your long-term savings needs to be kept in its own account where the money is safe, easily available to you in time of dire emergency, and subject to earning the highest rate of interest available.

Safety. You want your money safe from outside thieves, from accidental loss, but safe from you too. That means you don't want to keep it at home where making loans to yourself might be a little bit too tempting. You want your account in a federally insured bank or credit union, which protects your money from institutional failures, up to $250,000.

Availability. This requirement precludes you keeping your emergency fund in an investment vehicle like the stock market, collectibles, or other type of account that exposes it to risk and would require time to liquidate.

Interest-bearing. You want an account that is earning the best rate of interest possible, but not at the expense of your emergency fund being safe. You need to find an account with a higher rate than you'll get at the typical brick-and-mortar walk-in bank.

Online savings banks offer an excellent place for long-term savings. In fact, this is where you will find the so-called "high yield" rates. Online savings accounts meet the criteria I have stated above and add a fourth: convenience. Online savings banks offer free FDIC-insured accounts. These accounts are tied to your current checking account no matter where that bank is.

I am a huge fan of online savings banks and recommend that you use this for your Rule 2 savings because online banks offer simple banking, great rewards, convenience, and almost no hassles (no bank is perfect).

These days, as big banks are nickel-and-diming their customers with fees, fees, and more fees, online savings banks remain fee free. Interest rates are relatively higher than the big banks and customer service is far superior.

Online banks don't have tellers or branches so they have little overhead. That allows them to pay more interest and offer free accounts. The way that you access an online savings account is via the internet, or by mailing a deposit in a pre-addressed envelope.

How to Open an Online Savings Account

You don't have to switch banks to get the best savings account for your long-term savings. The way it works is that your online savings account gets linked to your current checking account, making transfers back and forth easy and very convenient.

If you have never banked online, you may be concerned about whether it's safe. Or you may be intimidated because it requires that you share your personal information online. Once you come to understand how to open a savings account online and discover the high-tech security measures these banks use, you will find it to be simple, at least as safe as a regular bank, and a rather convenient process.

Once you identify the internet bank where you want to open your account, you are ready to tackle opening an account. Generally, all of these banks follow the same steps to open an account.

When you visit the website of the online savings bank you have chosen, look around. You should see a button, link, or banner that prompts visitors to open an account. Click on it and you will see a form where you fill in your personal information, such as your name, address, email, phone number, and other identifying information. You will also be prompted to set up a log-on name and password to access your savings account online. As a standard procedure you will be asked to agree to the terms and conditions of the bank practices. Once you do this, you have completed the first step. Your account is now open.

ACTIVATE THE ACCOUNT

Account activation requires you to verify information to prove you are the person who just opened that account. It may be as simple as supplying the bank with your driver's license number or Social Security number. Some banks send a text message to the cell phone number you supply or to your email address with a request to reply to verify that you are the person who actually opened the account. Other banks may have a representative call you on the phone to verify the information verbally. It is typically a quick process whatever method is used.

Fund the Account

Once your account is open and active, you will be prompted to complete the information on how you intend to fund the account. Typically, you can link this new account to your existing checking account. Simply add the routing number and bank account number for another bank for that account, then transfer funds from one account into the other. It is a slick process. Or if you are more comfortable, you can mail in a check or money order to fund the account. Some banks now offer mobile deposit, which allows you to use your smart phone to make a check deposit and adds another layer of convenience.

It takes ten minutes or less to get an online savings account set up, activated, and running.

I am particularly fond of INGDirect for its user-friendly website, ease of use, and stellar customer service. They make it so easy to set up an account, transfer funds, and manage a savings account.

Here's how it works: go to INGDirect.com and open a new Orange Savings Account. You will need to give them your current checking account number and your bank's routing number (it's on the bottom of your checks—they show you where to find it). Once active, move some money from your checking account into your new savings account to get it started, and you're all ready to go.

Make It Automatic

Any time that you can automate your finances, do it. If you try to remember to transfer money into your Rule 2 account every payday, for example, you might remember, but chances are pretty good that you won't. Or you'll be a few days late. Automatic transfer is a superior option. Set it up by creating a regular automatic withdrawal from your checking account into your online savings account. It's simple and will allow you to put Rule 2 on autopilot.

First figure out the exact dollar amount you want transferred, rather than a percentage. That's simple enough. Just be careful when you select the date on which this automatic withdrawal will occur.

Let's say that you get paid $2,000 net on the 1st and again on the 15th of each month. Your paychecks are deposited directly into your regular checking account on those days. Don't set up your automatic transfer for the same day as you're paid. You want to allow for a little wiggle room in case payday falls on a holiday and to allow for other such delays. Create your automatic transfers of $200 each to occur on the 2nd and 16th, or a schedule you're comfortable with.

That's the way Rule 2 looks in action. Of course you can make manual transfers for other sources of income that may not be as predictable.

While you might miss the money for the first couple of months, I promise you that soon you won't even think about it. It will be like money that is deducted from your paycheck for taxes, FICA, and other items withheld. It's human nature to not miss what we don't see.

How Much to Save

Your emergency fund needs to contain at least enough money that you could pay all of your bills and monthly expenses for six months without a paycheck. The principle is this: if you become unemployed or for some other reason your income is temporarily cut off, you need to be prepared to take full responsibility for keeping all of your bills paid and your life intact until you can find another job. That's the kind of emergency that this account is for, not for buying new clothes or going on a fun weekend vacation.

So how much money are we talking about? It's different for every individual or family because it depends on your current expenses. Will you be eligible for unemployment benefits if you were to lose your job? Again, it all depends on the circumstances at the time.

You could take a lot of time to quantify and project, or you could simply multiply your current monthly expenses by six and consider that a good, round number for your emergency fund.

Consumer expenditure statistics from the US Department of Labor indicate that the average annual expenditure per consumer unit, which is similar to a household, is $49,067, as of 2009 (the most recent year for which data is available). Doing a little quick math in my head indicates the typical household needs $25,000 in cash reserves to be held for major emergencies.

While your household expenses may be higher or lower than the average, there's no doubt that even three months' worth of expenses is a big number ($12,500 for this average household).

If you currently have no savings to speak of, I wouldn't be surprised to hear you say, "I can't come up with that kind of money." I understand, but don't dismiss the possibility or the necessity too quickly. You really don't have a choice when it comes to preparing for the future. So let's figure out how you can do this, no matter your current situation.

Why So Much?

The amount of money required to fund a proper emergency fund is certainly significant. You might be tempted to dismiss the six months' expenses as overkill. But we live in uncertain times with uncertain economies. Corporate loyalty is a thing of the past, and unemployment can happen unexpectedly, usually at the worst possible moment. Likewise, emergencies can be expensive, and there's never a good time for these things to happen.

The secret to building your emergency fund is breaking it into bite-size goals. You wouldn't think of sitting down and eating an entire sausage in one gulp. But if you cut it into thin slices and take them one at a time, with enough time you really can eat the whole thing. The same principle works with any seemingly insurmountable task. Using the "sausage method," break it down into small slices and short goals.

How much would it take for you to keep your life together for two weeks without a paycheck? That should be a much smaller amount, and a goal that is easily achievable.

Once you reach the two-week mark, do a cartwheel, then go for three. Then a month, then two months. Soon you will be fully funded for the recommended six months and you'll be astonished by what you've accomplished.

Here's a small bonus you can look forward to: saving money can become addictive, and I do mean that in a good way. As your contentment grows and your fears subside, your confidence will soar. And your financial picture will begin to reflect this change of attitude and heart.

Saving 10 percent of your net income is a lifelong habit. You will always save the first 10 percent from any income that you receive, although you will not continue to funnel your savings into your emergency account. Once your emergency fund is fully funded at the level that you determine is right for you, your Rule 2 savings will have other jobs to do until eventually you are channeling the full 10 percent into investment vehicles that will speed up the time it takes for you to reach that crossover point where you reach financial freedom (see figure 4.5, page 47).

This Is a Must

No matter your situation—even if you are up to your eyeballs in credit card debt—you must have an emergency fund. Every household needs one. The very foundation of our money management plan is liquid cash, meaning that in 24 to 72 hours you could get your hands on money you have earmarked for specific emergencies. Without an emergency fund you will spin your wheels trying to get out of debt because every time something unexpected comes up, you'll feel you have no choice but to run for the credit cards. An emergency fund creates margin and allows you to step away from the edge.

Your attitude about your emergency fund will either make or break it. If you see it as a pool of money to be used at will for anything that suits your fancy at the moment, you have completely missed the purpose of an emergency fund. If and when the funds are used for the purpose for which they have been set aside, they must be quickly replaced. Maintaining an emergency fund provides much-needed space between you and the financial edge.

Supplement to Get Going

You may be anxious to get your emergency fund growing at a faster rate than 10 percent of your net income will allow. Good. Realistically, you need to save at least $1,000 as quickly as possible. Then keep going to $2,000 and on until you reach your goal.

To get there faster, find ways to dedicate $5 a day to the effort. Do that and you'll boost that account with an extra $1,825 in a year, or $9,125 in just five years.

Here are some other ideas for how you can supplement your efforts to get your emergency fund funded more quickly.

- Take the change out of your pockets at the end of the day and collect it in a jar.

- Stop spending $1 bills. Add them to the jar at the end of each day too. It's funny how in no time at all you won't miss them.

- Eat at home instead of dining out and tip yourself by adding a few bucks to your emergency fund.

- If you get "cash back," refunds, or rebates, or pay off a debt such as a credit card account or school tuition, put that newfound money into your emergency fund. If you get a tax refund, deposit the check into your fund.

- Sell stuff you don't need or want, to raise cash.

- Start thinking of your new emergency fund as you would an insurance policy. Guard it carefully. It's not a piggy bank. You should not be dipping into it for incidental expenses when you run short or get an urge to buy a new outfit or the latest in electronic gadgetry.

- Use it only for authentic emergencies—then hope that an emergency never happens. Remember, this fund is the new way that you finance your own emergencies. If you spend any of it, you must set up a way to re-place it, something that always takes much longer than anticipated.

6 Rule 3

Give Some Away

Nothing is enough for the man to whom enough is too little.
—Epicurus, Greek philosopher, 341–270 BC

Greed is our second financial enemy that will do all it can to make sure you never find contentment.

While Fear and Greed are so closely related you might tend to think of them as identical twins, they are distinctive in this way: Fear works to make you insecure about the future while Greed sabotages your present. Both of them will make you miserable if allowed to live freely in your life.

In this chapter we take on our most formidable enemy, Greed.

Rule 3: Give away some of your money out of a heart of gratitude, with no strings attached or expectation of anything in return.

Greed is a selfish and excessive desire to have more and more even without regard for whether you might already have enough or the cost to get more. It is that insatiable desire to have what others have whether you can afford it or not.

Greed drives you to do dumb things with your money and encourages you to become self-centered and self-serving.

Greed skews your thinking and makes you believe that if you can just get a bigger house or a newer car or that cool new electronic gadget, then you'll be satisfied.

Greed whispers in your ear that you are entitled to things you like, things you want, and things others have. Greed pushes you to respond to ads and offers impulsively without considering the consequences.

Greed vs. Contentment

Contentment says, "I am grateful for what I have, I want what I have, I have enough to satisfy."

Greed says, "More is not enough, I deserve even more, I want it all and I don't care what it takes to get it."

Contentment and greed cannot cohabitate. They cannot exist at the same time. One of them has to go. Greed must die for contentment to live.

Greed Is Never Good

When Gordon Gekko, the main antagonist in the 1987 film *Wall Street*, declared in no uncertain terms that "Greed is good!" people flocked to the theaters. And cheered. Please don't base your belief system on a movie line that might have been memorable and entertaining but dead wrong. Greed is like a cancer that when left untreated can destroy individuals, families, businesses, governments, and economies.

Greed makes financially ignorant people putty in the hands of the consumer credit industry. My ignorance about credit and debt and my skewed logic that somehow I could have all that I wanted now and it would somehow work out in the end, set me up to be greed's dream client. Credit was my accomplice.

I drove fancy new (leased) cars. I owned a beautiful cerulean mink jacket. I located the Steinway grand piano of my dreams and instructed the salesman to have it delivered. We took fancy vacations and bought expensive gifts. Our kids had all they could desire. But none of that was enough. I wanted a bigger home and newer cars.

Of course we didn't have any money to do all of this. So I blithely summoned Visa and MasterCard to bridge the gap between what I had and what I wanted. It didn't matter that we couldn't afford all of these things. If I wanted them, I got them, and the "afford" part would have to work itself out later.

Just think how marketing ploys like "No Interest, No Payments for a Year!" or "36 Easy Payments!" open the door to greed. They get our consumer engines revved up as we plan for how we'll get what we want now and skip all of that saving-the-money-first nonsense. By that time, whatever-it-is will have lost its glamour, so what's the point? Greed when exposed to available credit is a financial mistake just waiting to happen.

Greed is communicable. So you think that colds and flu are easily transferred between friends, family, and classmates? Nothing beats the way greed can spread, especially from parents to children.

By the time I made that U-turn on the highway to financial devastation, our two young boys were already showing signs of greed and dissatisfaction. My greed had spilled over to them. I started by being greedy for them, insisting that they have the best birthday parties and the best toys and clothes; that they were involved in all of the sports activities available in our area, and that they participated in every optional thing at school.

Christmas was an event to behold in our home as we lavished our boys with their every desire. Greed spread through our family like the flu bug. The only difference? It didn't go away on its own after a few days of bed rest. (You can read about the plan and the journey that took our boys from overly indulged children to financially confident men in my book *Raising Financially Confident Kids*.)

How serious is greed? Plenty, but don't take only my word for it. The Bible says that greed and the wanton desire to get rich is a temptation and a trap that can lead to ruin and destruction. It goes on to say that lust for money and possessions is a root of all kinds of evil, and can pierce one's heart with many griefs.[1] I know about ruin and destruction at the hand of a burning desire to become wealthy. I've had my heart pierced with grief as a result. If there is anything in this book that you are tempted to take lightly, please do not let it be the matter of greed.

Break the Grip of Greed

Breaking the stranglehold of greed starts with releasing the thing that has the power to consume you. Enter Rule 3. Giving away some of your money quiets your desires and knocks the life out of greed. Here are the steps to break the grip of greed.

1. Develop personal compassion. Putting others' needs ahead of our wants takes our eyes off of our selfish desires. It softens our hearts and fills us with compassion for the needs of others.

2. Develop generosity. A heart filled with gratitude expresses itself with generosity. Generosity kills greed. As you acknowledge all that you have in light of the needs of those around you, you'll find yourself feeling genuinely grateful in ways you may have not experienced before. Generosity will become the natural outflowing of your grateful heart.

3. Put others' needs ahead of your wants. Take some of your wants and find someone who has a real need. Take the money you would have spent on those wants and give it to the needy instead.

4. Repeat. Give some of your money away, systematically and regularly, as part of your personal money management program.

Giving is the way to break the grip of greed so that contentment can thrive.

Giving brings balance to your life. It is an effective antidote for the condition that has the potential to ruin your life, because it connects you to something greater than yourself.

Giving is the way that you express just how grateful you are for all that you have. Giving proves the condition of your heart. God promises to bless you in the same way that you bless others. It's like farming and the principles of sowing and reaping. If you sow sparingly, you're going to reap sparingly. If you sow generously, you will reap generously.

If giving is a new concept for you or one that you've never included in your life, you may be flooded with questions. Let me attempt to address the most common and perhaps obvious.

How Much to Give

How much you give is up to you, so don't look to me or others to tell you. Only you can make that determination. Your attitude is what will slay your enemy, greed. It's not how much you give, it's why you give. It's not the quantity of the gift, but rather the quality of the giver that makes a difference.

Knowing you the way I do—and I only make such an assumption because I know myself so well—your first thoughts when you read the preceding paragraph were "Great, then I'll give a dollar or two and call it good" or "I'll just wait until something or someone needy walks up and hits me in the head, then I'll give" or even "I'll give as soon as all my bills are paid and I get my money straightened out. But until then, I need every penny I can get my hands on."

No, no, and no. If you see your attitude in any of the foregoing, you don't understand Rule 3. You've missed the power of giving and a grateful heart.

This third money rule for your life is that you give away some of your income as you receive it, regardless of your life circumstances including your debt, outstanding bills, and any other needs and wants.

Practically, let me suggest that you come up with a percentage rather than a set fixed amount. When you receive a paycheck, inheritance, bonus, dividend, unemployment check, refund, gift, or any other channel through which God delivers money into your life, giving a percentage keeps it simple. As you are blessed with greater income, your giving will increase proportionately. As you go through lean seasons, your giving will adjust as well.

If you operate in an opposite manner where you wait until you happen to see a need somewhere and then you decide the amount you will give, you'll soon fall off that wagon. Take it from someone who knows.

The goal here is to establish a habit. The only way to do that is to repeat a behavior over and again until it becomes an almost automatic response.

Let me offer a money management shortcut that has worked like magic for me because it removes the guesswork: 10-10-80. This simple formula is quite possibly the best money management tool you can add to your personal finance tool belt, and it means: Save 10 percent, give 10 percent, then live on 80 percent of your net income. It's Rules 1, 2 and 3 rolled together into a simple formula that's nearly impossible to forget. Start applying this formula to the way you manage your money. Then repeat over and again. Before you know it, 10-10-80 will become a habit that will change your life in ways you may have never dreamed possible.

How to Give

Once you have established the amount—let's call it your Monthly Bless Others Budget—here are the five ways you should give.

1. Systematically. As you receive your income, take care of giving first before you do anything else including paying the bills, saving, loading up on groceries, or filling the gas tank. Take it right off the top. This leap of faith is an expression of your gratitude for this specific amount of money and also for all that you have, for all of the ways that you have been blessed, for all the comforts that you do enjoy, not the least of which is a place to live and food to eat. Remember, your attitude about giving is more important than the amount.

2. Thoughtfully. This is a deliberate decision that needs to be based on good plans. Your giving, like your spending, should not be impulsive or driven by emotion alone. It should be well thought out as part of your overall strategic plan.

3. Enthusiastically. You should never give out of guilt, or grudgingly. If you are not excited and engaged emotionally in the need that will be the focus of your gift, you may not have found the right place to give. Giving should stir up a sense of excitement for the good that your gift will do.

4. Voluntarily. Forced giving is useless. Giving induced by pressure from an organization, church, or individual can kill quickly the good that giving does in a person's life. Don't let anyone twist your arm into making a charitable donation. Don't give through clenched teeth or under duress. That does not represent a true, heartfelt desire to give out of a pure heart.

5. Cheerfully. Generosity brings happiness as sure as miserliness brings misery. As you give out of a heart of

gratitude, you're going to receive unbelievable joy. And that's going to make you happy to the point that you can't wait to give again. Generous, grateful people are happy people despite the challenging circumstances in which they may find themselves. In fact, giving allows them to rise above their circumstances.

Where to Give?

What are you passionate about? What stirs your heart? It's quite possible you know already where you will concentrate your giving. Perhaps you are part of a church. If you are being spiritually fed, it makes sense that you would want to help meet the financial needs right there in your church.

Start looking around in your own community. I'm quite certain that you won't have to look far to see genuine need that will engage you emotionally. You'll know because you'll feel a tug on your heartstrings. Once identified, get excited about how your giving will meet that need.

There's a delicate balance between giving without expectation of receiving anything in return and giving wisely. First recognize that there are scams out there posing as charitable nonprofit organizations serving the disenfranchised. Don't assume anything. Instead, make sure you have a good working knowledge of this organization or needy entity. This is the reason why giving locally has its benefits. You can see the church or the community center. You know the family who's cold or hungry, or you are impressed with the way your homeless shelter is reaching out to help battered women, abused children, or abandoned animals.

Look in your heart. What really matters to you? Let God turn that passion into compassion to guide you to a place of authentic need.

Power in Giving

More than a few people have asked me, "How on earth did you repay more than $100,000 in unsecured consumer debt and keep your life going at the same time?"

To tell you the truth, I am not sure how we did that, exactly. I wasn't taking notes because I never dreamed I would ever tell anyone what we were going through. It was embarrassing. But as I look back from where I am now, I can recall the many opportunities God provided for us to earn the money to repay the debt. And I have to admit that it is amazing.

What I do know is that day when I got up from the floor and gave my life over to God's care, I knew Scripture was pretty clear on this matter of giving. And I knew that I'd blown it big-time.

What I didn't know then was that God knows about my needs, he cares about my wants, and he wants to bless me. But it's dependent on my willingness to be obedient. It is an "if then" kind of thing. He says, "If you do this, then I will do that."

Here's my paraphrase of God's promises: "If you will obey me, then I will bless you. And the more I see that I can trust you, the more I will bless you. All I ask is that you give away part of everything I hand to you. I want you to care for the needy and bless those who are poor and hungry. Go ahead, test me on this if you think it might not be true. Just see if you can out-give me. As you are faithful to bless others, I will take care of you and provide for all of your needs. And more than that, once you prove that you are trustworthy, I will pour out a blessing on you that will be so great, you will not be able to hold all of it."[2]

We started giving to God and saving for the future from whatever money we received, even when we were deeply in debt. We tried hard to give and save consistently, even when it was in very small amounts. And one by one, the opportunities materialized. I got a job, which after three years led to us starting our own business. We moved into a new home, were able to provide for our two sons' educations, and we got out of debt.

In a way, I guess you could say that we gave and saved our way out of debt. That's the only explanation I have for how we paid back that enormous amount of debt including all of the interest, penalties, and fees. We didn't win the lottery or receive an inheritance. We accepted every opportunity, earned all we could, and just kept going for 13 long years until we reached the goal.

I cannot say that my battles with greed are over. That enemy has a way of lifting its ugly head when I least expect it. I know that I could so easily go right back to where I was if it were not for a mind-set of generous giving, a habit that changed the equation of my life. Giving has freed me from the stranglehold of materialism.

I have lived in the darkness of greed and debt. And I've lived on the receiving end of God's promise to reward trustworthiness. I highly recommend the latter.

7 Rule 4

Anticipate Your Irregular Expenses

> The essence of wise living is anticipating the unanticipated and expecting the unexpected.
>
> —Unknown

If I asked you to stop what you're doing, add up your monthly expenses, and deduct the total from your monthly income, I can nearly predict the result. You'd look up with a big smile on your face.

There it is right on that napkin (did I mention we're doing this over lunch?), proof that you spend less than you earn. Your income is greater than your outgo. You've nailed Rule 1. And I would be a bit nervous. At first glance, your list looks reasonably thorough. But it is not complete.

The mystery for many people is if their spending is so much lower than their income, why can't they get through an entire month without using credit to cover unexpected expenses, like medicine for a sick child, a semi-annual insurance premium, or a family birthday party?

Rule 4: Anticipate irregular expenses then prepare accordingly.

Most people, without actually thinking things through, assume their necessary expenses are those they pay each and every month. But not all necessary expenses recur as systematically as the rent, grocery bill, phone bill, and car payment. When we assume, however, that those are our only necessary expenses and allow them to grow to equal our income, everything falls apart when the nonrecurring, or "irregular," expenses show up.

Bills, expenses, and payments we make every month are generally not the problem. Somehow the rent and utilities get paid and the family gets fed. The problem is irregular expenses.

This is the way most of us think: the bills I paid this month are my necessary expenses. Everything else is optional. If an expense is not in my face at this moment, I have a choice whether to pay it or not. And if I have any money left at the end of the month I can spend it any way I want. The last thing on most of our minds in the middle of summer is Christmas. Who thinks about a major appliance breakdown or a big household repair somewhere out there in the future?

The solution for this problem is simple. You must become a money manager. If you don't know how to manage money, you've come to the right place. I am going to teach you how to do that here in Rule 4.

The purpose of Rule 4 is to plan ahead for irregular and even unexpected expenses in the same way you anticipate the expenses that you are keenly aware of because they happen every month. Of course this takes the foresight to look at an entire year rather than one month at a time. For example, I don't believe I have ever seen a person include Christmas gifts in their list of monthly expenses on the first go-round. And most people don't allow for clothes or family vacations when they do a quick tally of their routine expenses.

Here is the easiest way I know to implement both the anticipation aspect as well as the preparation required by Rule 4.

Determine what your irregular expenses are by looking at the past year. Look through your credit card statements and checkbook registers if you need a memory jog. You'll likely come up with things like car repairs, insurance (policies that are not paid monthly but rather quarterly or even once a year), summer camp, seasonal sports, and perhaps property taxes. Clothing may be an irregular expense you need to consider.

Next think about unexpected expenses that if you're really honest are probably not all that unexpected. You just don't know when they might hit. An example would be the deductible on your automobile collision insurance. Let's say it's $200 each year. What are the chances you'll need to come up with that? Slim to none, we hope. But just in case, wouldn't it be nice to know that money is safely tucked away? If you have pets, chances are pretty good that you're going to see a vet bill in the future. What were your pet costs in the last year? In the absence of a crystal ball, you could expect they'll be similar in the coming year.

Of course not all of our unexpected and irregular expenses need be so grim. If you're planning something special for an anniversary or planning to replace a piece of furniture or upgrade the decor in your bedroom, the money to pay for it is not likely to drop from the sky just in the nick of time. The way to deal with this is to anticipate.

I cannot tell you what joy and freedom Rule 4 will bring to your life. Anticipating then preparing accordingly brings with it a sense of maturity. You're a responsible grown-up. But it does require a good bit of planning followed by persistence.

Here's a Plan

Using records like your checkbook register, credit card statements, spending diaries, your tax return, or—if all else fails—your memory, make a list of your expenses over the last year that you didn't have every month. It might be insurance, property taxes, gifts, clothing, vacation, Christmas, car repairs, sports, hobbies, etc. Come up with an annual figure (a guesstimate) for each and then divide by 12 to arrive at a monthly average.

Here's an example that addresses six irregular expenses that are highly predictable.

Description	Annual	Per Month
Auto Maintenance	$700	$58
Vet for Pets	$480	$40
Christmas	$1,000	$83
Property Taxes	$2,000	$166
Vacation	$1,500	$125
Gifts	$600	$50
Total	$6,280	$522

The way to "prepare accordingly" given this scenario is to treat $522 as a new fixed monthly expense. Refer back to Rule 2 and open a second online savings account. Once you have an account in place (you do, right? You opened one when we covered Rule 2, I'm just sure of it), it's simple to add a second account that will keep your reserve funds for irregular expenses separate.

Next, create an automatic withdrawal for $522 each month, or split it in half and make two automatic orders to transfer this money from your checking account. Automation is the secret.

As I said earlier, you'll feel a pinch the first few months. This will feel like a big new expense with nothing to show for it. But that is not at all true. All you'll need to do is click over to your online savings account and view the wonder of anticipating your irregular and unexpected expenses. And here's an extra nice thing. Since you are the manager, you can add and amend categories and transfer amounts as often as you need until you get this just right.

And as you get raises or bonuses in the future, consider adding categories and deposit amounts to reflect other irregular expenses or even "dream" savings. You could easily add a category like "Caribbean Cruise" or "computer," then fund it accordingly.

You will discover that by transferring these funds into a separate account, you will not be so tempted to borrow them back the way you might if you were to leave the money in your checking account, intending to not touch it.

Apply this kind of advance planning to all of the irregular expenses in your life, and those that could be considered unexpected, e.g., new washer and dryer. I can nearly guarantee that sometime in the future you will need to replace them or some other major home appliance. At the risk of sounding redundant, I will say it again: prepare accordingly.

If you believe that you are not able to implement Rule 4 because you don't have enough money or, more likely, you don't sense the urgency because you have other things you'd like to do with your money right now, we need to sit down and have a talk.

You're acting as if maintaining your auto is optional or you can skip paying your insurance if you're a little short. If you don't have money to put toward those coming expenses now, what makes you think you'll have it next month? It's not as if you have a choice whether to maintain your car, pay your property taxes, or buy clothes. But, you are driving a car, you paid your taxes, and you dress fairly well. Exactly how did you do that? You came up with the money somehow, and you probably have a few battle scars or credit card payments that help you remember the trouble you went through to do it. If you are covering your irregular expenses with a credit card, that's a huge problem.

Anticipating your irregular expenses is too important to pass off as something you cannot afford. You can't afford not to. I suggest you start out with a minimum number of categories, limiting them to your most essential irregular expenses. For example, you may have a property tax bill due in three months. That's essential. It's coming. You may have to reduce your spending in other areas in order to accumulate money for this item.

Whatever the sacrifice, no matter how painful to get it going, applying Rule 4 will change your life. It's one of the nicest things you will ever do for your finances and peace of mind. This is what money managers do. They manage money.

8 Rule 5

Tell Your Money Where to Go

> It is oftener the trifling outlays frequently repeated that prove ruinous than any conspicuous extravagance.
>
> —*Good Housekeeping* magazine, January 1900

If the word *budget* is like nails on a chalkboard, you've got a friend in me. I know that feeling.

For many years I wouldn't have anything to do with a budget because I couldn't stand the idea of someone who didn't know me or my situation telling me how to spend my money. That's how I defined a budget. It was a whip disguised as a formula with every intent of beating me into submission. And where did this sort of thinking get me? Into one big financial mess, because every month when we ran out of money I turned to MasterCard and Visa for a bailout. Bad idea.

What I learned from going through that experience and finding my way back to solvency is that a budget is the ticket to financial happiness, not the straitjacket I feared it would be. Still, I don't like the word, so if it's okay with you, let's drop the b-word and replace it with Rule 5. There. So much better.

Rule 5: Tell your money where to go, then make sure it gets there.

Like a road map or the blueprints for your dream house, a Spending Plan shows where you are and how to get where you want to be. A Spending Plan is like strapping on a set of wings and learning to fly.

In its simplest form, a Spending Plan is a sheet of paper on which you write your income for the coming month and what you will do with every dollar of it. You "prespend" your paycheck on paper before you part with any of it. Think of it as a dress rehearsal where you sit down with your money and you tell it where to go.

Creating a Spending Plan

A good Spending Plan addresses every bit of income by giving every dollar a specific job to do. Some will be directed to pay the rent or mortgage payments, others will be assigned to food, utilities, and right down the line through your bills. Some will fulfill your Rule 2 long-term savings account, others will go to work hard in your Rule 3 giving, while some of those dollars will bring balance to your life as they are assigned to entertainment and fun. Still others of your hard-earned dollars will follow your orders by heading to hiding places like retirement accounts and investments where they will be kept in reserve. A good Spending Plan becomes a great predictor and leaves a lot less to chance.

The purpose of a Spending Plan is not to force you into a life of deprivation but rather to prevent overspending, which will keep you from falling into debt. It rarely matters what you're overspending on—dining out, entertainment, clothes. In the end it's all debt.

Your Spending Plan is yours alone. You won't find one that I have designed for you on the following pages. And once you've made your first Spending Plan, it's not set in stone. You can change your mind, make minor tweaks, or toss it out and start all over again.

There is something startling about seeing your exact income and expenses for a full month laid out on paper. The exercise we did "over lunch" for Rule 4 was so loose, it could hardly be considered accurate. In Rule 5 you deal with accurate income, expenses, and spending.

If you have not done something like this before, let me warn you: rarely does a person's planned spending match actual spending exactly. In fact, in the first few months you may find your income and your recorded outgo to be from different planets! But do not despair. Think of this like working a jigsaw puzzle. When you dump out all the pieces, it looks like a big mess. But one piece at a time it starts to take shape. And the more patience and diligence you expend, the clearer your financial picture becomes and the greater your reward.

Once you have it just the way you want it, your Spending Plan becomes a handy road map that keeps your finances on track.

Grab a sheet of paper or sit down at your computer, and let's get started.

Step 1: Income

Write down your total household take-home monthly income. Because many expenses are billed monthly, you will find it easier to calculate your income this way so it matches most of your bills. Regardless of how you get paid—weekly, biweekly, twice a month, monthly—to come up with an average monthly figure, multiply your paycheck by the number of paychecks in a year and then divide by 12. Or, for a more precise number use the table below.

How to Determine Your Average Monthly Income

If you are paid . . .	Perform this calculation to get Average Monthly Income
Weekly	Multiply your weekly income by 4.333
Biweekly	Multiply your biweekly income by 2.167
Semimonthly	Multiply your semimonthly income by 2
Quarterly	Divide your quarterly income by 3
Annually	Divide your annual income by 12

When determining your average monthly income, include all sources such as salary, wages, commission, dividend and interest income, child-support payments, alimony, etc. If you get it on a regular basis, can predict its arrival, and can spend it, it's income.

Step 2: Essential Fixed Expenses

Write down your expenses. Start with your fixed bills like your Rule 2 Saving, Rule 3 Giving, Rule 4 Reserve Payment, rent, mortgage payment, car payment, credit card payments (if any), insurance, and other monthly expenses that are about the same every month. Include things like music lessons for the kids. While those may not be essential to the sustenance of life, they are things you consider necessary. These are your essential fixed expenses.

Step 3: Essential Variable Expenses

Next, list your essential variable expenses. These are bills you have every month but the amount varies from one month to the next. Examples would be your utilities, food, household expenses, gasoline, medication, public transportation, shoes and clothing. You can assign an estimated amount to each based on past experience, rounding to the closest $10.

Step 4: Non-essential Expenses

Next list reasonable amounts for non-essential expenses like entertainment, eating out, hobbies, and other ways you spend money in a typical month. This is the fun stuff. No matter how tight things are, it would be a mistake to eliminate fun and entertainment from your life entirely.

Step 5: Miscellaneous Monthly Expenses

Look at your checkbook register and credit card statements—or reports if you use financial software or electronic tracking—for the past several months to find any expenses you've left out.

Step 6: And the Total Is . . .

Add your expenses to come up with a single monthly number, then subtract from your income. If you come out with a positive number, this is a good sign, and indicates that you are not living beyond your means. Keep in mind that you may not have yet captured all of your expenses and typical monthly spending. But this is a great start.

If, on the other hand, your expenses exceed your income (a negative number is clear evidence of this problem), don't panic. Your Spending Plan will fix this. Most people discover that if it weren't for their monthly credit card debt payments, they would be spending less than they bring in. So the good news is that once you get rid of that debt, your financial picture is going to improve dramatically. But until then, it's time to sharpen the pencil.

Step 7: Cut, Adjust, Tweak, Repeat

If you came up short, go back and see where you can start cutting. Look first at your non-essential expenses. Which items can you remove for a while (eating out seems like a fine target, or perhaps hobby expenses)?

Where can you cut back without eliminating a spending category altogether? Keep going through the list, making adjustments until your total expenses are less than your income (see Rule 1). If you're living a lifestyle that requires all or more than your income, something has gone wrong. You are living at a level you cannot sustain. Keep working at it until your expenses are less than your income. Wisdom will dictate where you can cut the deepest.

Step 8: Track Your Spending

Hire yourself as project manager to implement your plan. You are the best person for the job because no one cares as much about your financial future as you do. Embrace it, get excited, and whatever you do, don't sit back and fall asleep on the job.

Keep track of your spending every day to see how closely you can live according to your plan. Write down everything, including the $2.99 smartphone app, the $.99 music file, the sodas from the vending machine, highway tolls, and parking fees in addition to the checks you write, debit card transactions, and any automated payments you have set up. Many people are astonished by how much they spend on stuff they thought didn't matter—fast-food restaurants, tools, gadgets, shoes, games, beauty salons, Costco, kids' expenses to name a few. Take notes and research ways you will be able to do even better next month. At month's end, add your actual spending and compare it to what you planned. Regardless of the outcome, you should be proud because you have taken such a big step toward your financial freedom. Most people don't have a clue what their true monthly income is or any idea where it all goes. Then, use this information to create next month's improved Spending Plan.

Congratulations! Just by creating a Spending Plan, you have moved from clueless to savvy. Your financial IQ is rising by the day. You should feel very good about this. As difficult as it might be to see in black and white if your income and expenses are not quite in sync, knowing where you are right now will make all the difference. It takes discipline to stick to a Spending Plan, and that's what builds character.

Even if you find yourself in a particularly tight financial position right now, take heart. As you pay off debts and find more ways to cut expenses, you'll begin to notice a significant decrease in financial pressure.

The sooner you get started creating a Spending Plan, the sooner you'll be on your way to reaching financial freedom. Start today—your future depends on it!

Helpful Hints and Tools

You need to create a "written" Spending Plan. There are many ways to do that. I suggest you choose the method that appeals to you.

At the very least, you'll need paper, pencil, and a basic calculator to track your spending throughout the month. You will find a Spending Plan template on page 110 that you can customize to fit your situation perfectly. Note the side-by-side columns "Last Mo." and "This Mo." I like this because it allows me to see my actual spending from last month compared to what I plan to spend this coming month in that particular category.

There are countless tips, tricks, and budgeting tools that will help you create the perfect Spending Plan and tracking methods. Some are available to you to download to your computer. What you are looking for is a method and tools that click for you.

Let me caution you that if the planning and tracking methods you select are too complicated, the process will become cumbersome and you won't stick with it. On the other hand if it is too general (most of your spending designated as "Miscellaneous"), it will be too vague to be effective.

Once you have your Spending Plan in place, you need an easy way to implement this plan. Here are some tools and ideas to get started.

Envelopes. This is a simple method of managing cash that you can team with your Spending Plan. First, get some envelopes. Then, write a spending category on each one and fund it with the amount you have allotted. Example: groceries—$250. As you buy groceries throughout the month, spend from this envelope only. Record the "What?" and "How much?" right on the envelope. The envelope creates a handy place to collect receipts as well. When the envelope is empty, no more grocery shopping until the next fill up. Do the same for things like gasoline, entertainment, fast food, and so on.

Reset your due dates. It can be a problem if all of your big bills come due about the same time, but you get paid twice a month. Here's an easy solution: call these companies and ask them to change your due date so due dates are spread in a way that works best with how you get paid. Most companies are happy to do this.

Automate. Sending checks through the mail has become slow, dangerous, and unreliable. Sign up for your bank's online bill payment system so you can utilize online bill pay and automatic payments.

Online bill pay. Here's how it works: you authorize money to be transferred from your bank account to your creditor's account. You do this all online through online access to your bank account. It's easy, user-friendly, and safe (transactions are encrypted). You can see immediately that you made the payment, plus your online account organizes your records and receipts. It is very cool and will simplify your financial life.

Automatic payments. Most lenders, utilities, and other regular billers offer auto-bill pay without any kind of fees. In fact, some lenders and others give you a break on the interest rate if you will agree to auto pay. The way it works is that you authorize a specific creditor to take your payment automatically from your checking account every month. You still get your statements and bills in advance, but your account does the work for you.

Pad your account. Putting your bills on "autopilot" is an effective way to simplify your finances. But you have to make sure that you always have enough in the bank to cover payments that will be made automatically. Here's an easy and effective way to vanquish any fears you might have of overdrafting your account and racking up huge fees and penalties: pad your checking account. A pad is a sum of money that you keep in the account but don't spend. In fact, you don't even include it in your current balance. Start with $100 then increase it from there, according to your comfort level. Think of the pad as another bit of insurance you have in place. If something happens out of your control and you go over your "official" balance, you won't incur any fees or penalties, but you will reduce the pad. Just make sure you restore the pad as quickly as possible. If you keep track of your balance online or via an ATM, you'll have to mentally deduct the $100 or amount of your pad.

Home Budget Calculator.[1] Bankrate.com offers a free calculator that shows you where your money is going. By entering income and monthly expenditures, you can quickly see how you are doing compared to Bankrate's standards and also see areas for improvement. Cost: free.

Mvelopes Personal.[2] This online service links with your bank and uses envelope icons to apportion your paycheck and keep track of spending. A virtual version of the old-fashioned envelope method (where you cash your paycheck, then divvy it up into envelopes that are labeled with spending categories like Rent, Food, etc.), Mvelopes gives you a visual cue of how much you've spent and how much money remains in each of your spending envelopes. If you go over in any category, the line item turns red. Cost: about $8 a month.

Mint.[3] This service sets up your budget online based on your average monthly spending. It then pulls all your financial accounts into one place. Set a budget, track your goals, and do more with your money. Once each week you receive an email that lists your current balance(s), suggestions for changes you might want to make, and tells you when bills are due. Cost: free.

Pear Budget. Not ready for a full-on money-management program that links to all of your financial accounts? You might be more comfortable with a program like *PearBudget .com*, which offers an excellent spreadsheet to help you track your spending. Cost: $4.95 per month.

Clear Checkbook. Another option is *ClearCheckbook .com*, an extremely easy-to-use tool that helps you balance your checkbook and manage your money. Think of Clear Checkbook as an online checkbook register with the added bonus of viewing reports, setting budgets, creating reminders, and more. Cost: free for the standard version or $4 per month for premium.

Quick & Easy Budget Kit CD.[4] Available only in Windows format, this four-step budgeting system may be exactly what works for you. At this writing it is free to download.

Monthly Spending Plan

Spending Category	Week 1 Days 1–7		Week 2 Days 8–14		Week 3 Days 15–21		Week 4 Days 22–End		Total Plan to Spend This Mo.	Total Actually Spent This Mo.	Total Spent Last Mo.
	Plan	Actual	Plan	Actual	Plan	Actual	Plan	Actual			
TOTALS											

9
Rule 6

Manage Your Credit

Now more than ever—knowing how to fix, improve, and protect your credit score are essential skills for successfully navigating your financial life.

—Liz Pulliam Weston

I'll admit it. This is not my favorite of the 7 Rules. Honestly, I would much rather change this rule to "Death to Credit, Live on Cash" and be done with it. But unless we can figure out how to turn back the clock a half century or so, that would be unwise, even foolish.

That leaves us with two choices. We can ignore the matter of consumer credit and just hope for the best (not a very good option) or take full responsibility for maintaining an excellent credit rating for the purpose of saving money and improving our financial intelligence and our effectiveness as money managers. We have to opt for the latter because your credit rating plays a very important role in your financial health.

Rule 6: Manage your credit rating to achieve a high level of creditworthiness.

Please read this rule again, paying close attention to the words "credit rating" and "creditworthiness." This rule does not mean going into debt, creating debt, or taking on huge sums of available credit.

Credit Is Not the Enemy

Credit on its face is not bad. In fact, having a good credit rating, which is measured by your credit scores, simply means that based on your past behavior, lenders, car rental companies, and others that you deal with can expect the same from you in the future. A high score is one of your most valuable money management tools for reasons we'll discuss in a bit. Just let me be perfectly clear that credit, like other things in life, has the potential for both good and bad. If abused, your access to credit can ruin your life. This is where financial maturity becomes an important asset.

As much financial trouble as I managed to get into because I abused credit cards and ran up insane amounts of toxic debt, I don't blame credit. I take responsibility for the foolish decisions I made and the horrific ways that I abused consumer credit. That my credit led to toxic debt was of my own doing.

Growing Misinformation

There is a trending belief in some circles that to have good credit you have to be in debt,[1] or that a credit report is just a "debt report" because it measures your debt. That is not true. You do not have to be in debt to be found highly creditworthy. As you will soon learn, there are ways to build your credit score that do not involve debt.

With so much misinformation going around, it's no wonder that consumer credit has become such a mysterious and complex subject.

Why You Need to Be Creditworthy

Without good credit, it's difficult to buy a home or qualify for the best insurance rates. The practice is called "risk-based pricing" and it is perfectly legal. A growing number of companies check credit reports before making hiring decisions. Landlords want to see a clean credit report before deciding who gets the apartment.

Like it or not, banks, credit unions, credit card companies, and auto financing companies look to credit data to set interest rates. Most banks now require a credit check to open a checking account.

Insurers, employers, property management companies, and even car rental companies assume that you will treat their property and conduct your business with them the way you've handled things in the past. Whether it's fair or not, a prospective employer can conclude that if you are sloppy with your own finances, you might be sloppy on the job. With so many candidates to choose from, why hire someone with lousy credit? With so many people wanting to rent that townhouse, why approve someone who has a history of paying late? The theory when it comes to creditworthiness is that your past behavior predicts your future behavior.

These days a poor credit rating can be costly, and that's the reason you need to assume the role as your own personal credit manager.

What follows may appear at first glance as just technical stuff worthy of skipping over. Please do not do that.

To get up to speed quickly on this matter of maintaining a good credit rating, you need to be familiar with a few terms.

Credit reporting agency (CRA). A company that gathers consumer credit related information from banks, credit unions, public records, inquiries, department stores, property management companies, and others, then compiles it and sells it back to consumers, lenders, insurance companies, employers, and other businesses that have a legitimate business purpose for the information as individual credit reports. The three major CRAs are Equifax, Experian, and TransUnion.

Credit report. This is all of the information associated with your name and Social Security number that a CRA has in its credit file. This information can change monthly as new information is reported and gathered by the CRA. Negative information can be reported for seven to ten years (depending on the nature of the negative item) while positive information is reported indefinitely.

Credit score. This is a three-digit number that judges how well you handle credit over time. It is based on the contents of your credit report and rates the possibility that you won't pay your bills in the future. While you have many credit scores, the one lenders use is the FICO score, so don't waste your time or money on any others. Each of the credit bureaus has a FICO score for you, which is based on the information in their credit file.

How to Manage Your Creditworthiness

These are the three credit-related instruments you need to monitor on a regular basis to manage your credit rating:

1. Your credit report
2. Your credit score
3. Your credit card account

Your Credit Report

Each of the big three CRAs has a credit report on you, and you need to monitor each of them closely, once each year. Think of your credit reports as rap sheets. They contain allegations made by others about you and the way you handle credit and pay your bills. That information may or may not be true. I can promise you that no one but you cares one way or the other about accuracy in your report. If it contains incorrect negative information, it could be costing you dearly in higher insurance premiums or interest rates. That is why it is so important that your credit report contains only true and accurate information.

By federal law, you have a right to know what the credit bureaus have in their files about you so that you can confirm that the information is true and correct, make corrections, or dispute an item altogether.

The law requires each of the big three CRAs to give you one copy of their credit report on you, free of charge, every

12 months. You can get all three of your reports at once or order from one bureau now, another in four months, the third four months after that. This way you will stay current year-round with what is being reported to the bureaus about you.

It can be a little tricky to get your free reports, so make sure you highlight the following information. Do not go directly to any one of the CRA websites or call them directly to get your free annual credit report. It won't work, you'll get frustrated, and you might even get tricked into paying for it.

The only way you can get your free reports is to start at AnnualCreditReport.com (or call 1-877-322-8228 to request your credit report by phone). This is the official site that complies with the federal law and the only place you can start the process to get your free reports. Once at this site, follow the prompts. You will have to reveal your name and Social Security number (don't worry, they already have it) and other personal identifying information.

If you are able to identify yourself to the satisfaction of each CRA by correct responses to security questions, you can get your free credit report within a few minutes, downloaded to your computer. If not, you will be instructed to call a toll-free number to speak with a customer service agent. You will also find instructions for how to proceed if you prefer to receive your free credit report by mail.

Once you have your credit report in hand, remember what I said about this being a kind of rap sheet. These are allegations that others have made about you. Your job now is to make sure that the information is accurate.

Check everything from the spelling of your name to your address and all other personally identifying information. Industry estimates are that 70 percent of all credit reports contain errors. It's hard to imagine how any entity could survive with a 30 percent accuracy rate, but that's what they tell us, so expect to find some kind of error. Be especially wary if you happen to share a name with a parent, e.g., your father is Sr. and you are Jr. Family data can get mixed up, particularly when people share the same name or address.

Look at every single entry. Do you recognize the name and account numbers of the accounts that allegedly belong to you? The report says you were 30 days late with a payment four years ago. Is that correct? As you go through line by line, make a note of anything you do not recognize or do not know to be true. Just because there is something on your report that is negative does not make it true. By law you can have incorrect information removed from your credit file by following the dispute instructions that will come with your report. You should pursue that immediately if you find errors.

Your FICO Scores

Unlike credit reports, FICO scores are not free. You have to buy them. You can purchase your FICO scores from Equifax and TransUnion through MyFICO.com. Experian does not make its FICO score available to consumers. At this writing, FICO scores are $15.95 each.

While it is important that you review each of your credit reports at least once a year, I see no similar need to check your credit score that often. Your credit score is a measurement of what's in your credit reports. If you are monitoring your reports well, your score will take care of itself.

Unlike your credit reports, there is no process by which you can correct, change, or dispute your FICO scores. So, there's really no need to spend money to get your credit score more often than annually, if then, unless you are planning to apply for a mortgage or finance a car in the coming year. If you are, you (and your spouse or co-borrower) should begin monitoring your FICO score now. If you find that your score is lower than necessary to get the best rates, you may have time to improve. It would be highly appropriate to call a lender ahead of time to find out what FICO score they require to get their best rates.

What is a good FICO score? Before the US economy crashed in 2007, a FICO score of 720 was considered excellent. Since then, lenders have tightened their standards, requiring much stricter criteria in their assessments of creditworthiness. This is how lenders assess FICO scores today:

620 = Minimum

720 = Good

760 = Great

780 = Excellent

What's in Your Score[2]

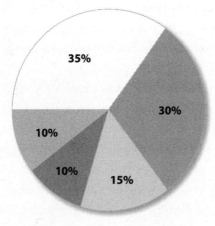

Payment History 35%
Utilization Rate 30%
Longevity 15%
Inquiries 10%
Credit Mix 10%

Much of what goes into determining a FICO score remains guarded trade secrets. However, we do know that there are five categories that make up the "points" in your FICO credit scores.

Payment history, 35 percent. This category, which is the most important, counts for 35 percent of your score and reflects how you pay your bills. You get the most points if you never pay late and you have no negative entries like bankruptcy, judgments, tax liens, charge-offs, collections, repossessions, foreclosures, settlements, or excessive late payments in your credit file. If you do have negative entries, they weigh heavily if they occurred in the past two years. Negative information will remain in your file for seven to ten years, depending on what it is. Positive information, however, remains forever.

Amounts owed, 30 percent. This data looks at how much you currently owe compared to how much of your available credit you are using currently. This ratio is known as your "utilization rate." The more of your available credit that you are using at any given time, the more risky you are. FICO wants to see that you have available credit, but then gives you points for not using it. A great utilization rate is below 10 percent. Example: you have a credit card with a $2,500 limit. You should never use more than $250 of that limit, which would be 10 percent utilization (because $250 ÷ $2,500 = .1), to score well in this category. You will get the maximum points if you carry no debt, meaning your utilization rate is 0 percent.

Length of credit history, 15 percent. This category gives points for how long you have had a credit account, even if you consistently maintain a $0 balance. The longer you have had a credit line, the better. Your oldest credit card becomes your most valuable because of its longevity.

Credit inquiries, 10 percent. Every time you apply for new credit, it shows up as an inquiry. An inquiry can be for a loan, cell phone service, or a new credit card. An inquiry is logged when you apply for instant credit at a retail store or grant access to your credit file to a prospective employer or landlord. Inquiries are considered negative and will pull your score down. Some lenders automatically turn down anyone with three or four inquiries over a short period of time. Inquiries remain in your credit file for up to two years. To get the most points in this category, FICO wants to see only a couple of inquiries at the most in the past two years.

There are exceptions: (1) when you request a copy of your own credit report or credit score, it is not recorded as an inquiry and (2) if you are shopping for a new mortgage or car loan, all inquiries you make within a 14-day period will count as just one application or inquiry. Make sure you keep your shopping within that time frame.

Mix of Credit, 10 percent. This is the mixture of the accounts that you have such as revolving lines of credit, installment loans, mortgage, and vehicle loans. Consumers with a combination of these accounts are considered less risky than those with just one type. FICO believes that account diversity is good.

Your Credit Account

To have a credit rating you do need to use credit. But you do not have to carry credit card *debt*. You do not have to pay interest to build a great credit rate. All you need is one major credit card (not a debit card) with which you make a purchase three times a year. A $10 purchase that you pay off immediately will fulfill the requirement of "using credit."

The High Cost of Poor Credit

The contrast in score-based interest rates between consumers with low credit scores and those with high scores is becoming starker than ever on many loans for mortgages, cars, and other consumer products. The bottom line is that poor credit could cost you hundreds of thousands of dollars over your lifetime.[3]

The following information[4] shows how much a monthly car payment on a fixed-rate 36-month loan of $10,000 will vary depending on your FICO score. In this example two people with exactly the same income and life situation apply for the loan. The only difference is their FICO scores.

How It Pays to Have a Good Credit Score

FICO Score	Annual Percentage Rate	36-Month Auto Loan
720-850	4.261%	$296
690-719	5.720%	$303
660-689	7.769%	$312
620-659	11.282%	$329
590-619	16.338%	$353
500-589	17.883%	$361

Interest rates accurate as of July 26, 2011

The person with the high FICO score will repay $10,656 ($296 x 36 = $10,656), while the one with the low FICO score will repay a total of $12,996 ($361 x 36 = $12,996). The high cost of a low score in this example is a whopping $2,340. Now who says credit scores don't matter?

How to Kill Your FICO Score

If by some bizarre turn of events you decide that you'd like to trash your credit rating by dropping hundreds of points from your excellent FICO score of, let's say, 780 (I am not actually suggesting that you should do any of these, but just pretend along, okay?), here are five ways you could do that.

1. Max out a credit card account. That's right. If your credit limit is, for example, $2,500, make sure your outstanding balance is right at $2,499. This should produce a dramatic plunge of at least 45 points for achieving 100 percent utilization.
2. Pay late. Go ahead and procrastinate on making that minimum monthly payment. In fact, if you can possibly hold out, wait for 30 days so your lateness gets reported to all of the CRAs and you will enjoy a healthy drop of 110 points.
3. Settle. Gather all your courage and call your credit card company or other lender to whom you've become a problem payer. Let them know about the $5,000 you won last week with that lucky scratch-off lottery ticket. See if they'll accept that as settled payment for your current balance, which is more than double that amount. They will? Must be your lucky day. Do it. Pay them off and watch them report your account to the CRAs as "settled" (one of the kisses of death to a credit report, just above

"foreclosure" and "bankruptcy"). Then go ahead and log another 125-point drop on your FICO score.

4. Just walk away. It's not your fault that the value of your home has dropped below the amount you owe on the mortgage. You never liked the house anyway, so do what your friends say they've done: walk away! Well, don't really walk, but just stop making the payments. Who knows how long it will take the lender to foreclose and serve you the proper legal notice to leave? At least you won't have to make the payments every month while you are a bona fide squatter on the property. Once "foreclosure" shows up in your credit file, you can lop another 160 points from your FICO score.

5. Clean the slate. Things are so messed up for you, don't you deserve a fresh, clean start? Go ahead and file for bankruptcy. After all, your FICO score is so shot, what difference will another 240 points make? Just kill the darned thing and put it out of its misery. Besides, the next ten years are just going to fly by given the three jobs you'll have to work to claw your way back from the pit of financial despair and a FICO score of 100.

Okay, enough with the sarcasm. Let's take a look at the things you can do to push your FICO scores up to that excellent range.

How to Improve Your FICO Score

1. Pay your bills on time, all the time. Never incur late or over-limit penalty fees.

2. At the minimum, use one credit card three times a year to make a small purchase, then pay the balance down to $0 immediately.
3. If you carry any other credit card debt, reduce your credit utilization rate on single accounts as well as your accounts combined, as quickly as possible. A utilization rate below 30 percent is acceptable, 10 percent is better, 0 percent utilization is best.
4. Refrain from closing accounts if doing so will increase your utilization rate because you will be losing available credit.
5. Refrain from opening new accounts. Even though it might make sense that opening new lines of credit you don't intend to use will improve your utilization rate, the opposite is true. FICO scoring interprets new credit as an intention to go into debt.

A Final Word on Credit Cards

You may assume that given my financial history and the way that credit card debt nearly ruined my life, that I wouldn't carry a credit card even if my life depended on it and that I recommend you get out the scissors to perform a little plastic surgery. If that is the case, I am about to disappoint.

I am not patently opposed to credit cards. They're essential to use online, to rent a car or book a hotel room, or to buy a plane ticket. If your card has no annual fee and a 20-day interest-free grace period for paying the balance before interest accrues, you're getting free monthly loans. What I am against is buying more on your credit card than you can easily pay for at the end of the month. That's the threshold. That's the point of danger. If you are ever unable to pay the balance in full, allowing a balance to roll over to the following month, that is a red flag. You have abused that card and the result is high-interest, toxic debt. You need to stop using the card for anything until you pay that balance in full.

The truth is that a credit card—the right credit card—used smartly by someone with a modicum of financial intelligence can be a useful financial tool that can also contribute to a high FICO score.

Card criteria. Every adult, or household, should have a good, all-purpose credit card that is used carefully and in a way that does not create debt. You don't need multiple credit cards. One is sufficient to build and maintain a good credit score and offer a great deal of consumer protection. This card should be a MasterCard or Visa with no annual fee, 20-day interest-free grace period, and a low interest rate.

Purchase protection. Federal law provides a great deal of consumer protection for purchases made with a credit card. If that item doesn't show up or if it's not what you ordered or turns out to be defective, you are covered. The credit card company will investigate and reverse the charges to your account.

Unauthorized use. If your card is stolen or in any way used without your authorization, you pay nothing provided you report the loss before any fraudulent charges show up. Even if a charge is not reported in a timely manner, what you pay cannot exceed $50 regardless of the fraudulent amount.

10 Rule 7

Borrow Only What You Know You Can Repay

Our self-centered, debt-centered economy is like those electronic bug-zappers. They emit a light attractive to insects that blissfully fly right into the trap, only to be killed.

—Randy Alcorn

Given the number of people who lost their homes through foreclosure when the US housing market crashed, setting off the Great Recession, it would be easy to conclude that borrowing money to purchase a home is way too dangerous, fiscally foolish, and to be avoided.

We could take a similar stance on financing a car or taking student loans because automobiles depreciate and there are no guarantees of jobs for college grads.

We could flat-out ban borrowing money in our lives, but that would be like the proverbial throwing the baby out with the bathwater.

I am grateful for a home mortgage. Without it, my husband and I would not have had a prayer of owning our home. And I don't believe that financing an automobile is evil or that all student debt is toxic. Rule 7 insures you have a safety net when borrowing money.

Borrowing money and the debt that creates should be taken on rarely, and then dealt with swiftly. Debt should be a means to an end. Borrowing money is a financial tool that improves your life if dealt with intelligently, not emotionally.

Rule 7: Borrow only what you know you can repay.

When I use the word "know," I do not mean with absolute certainty beyond a reasonable doubt know. I mean to know as in having a reasonable certainty based on credible information. Another way to put it would be "borrow only what you have a reasonable certainty based upon credible information that you can repay," which seems awkard. So let's stick with "know" in this rule, knowing that we know what it means.

The only way that you can know with a reasonable level of certainty that you can pay off a debt is to have the means to do so in reserve. That goes for every type of borrowing, every kind of debt. This is so important, I am going to repeat it: the only safe way to borrow money is to have a means to pay off the debt in reserve.

The Trouble with Debt

Debt is not ideal. It's not a prize you get for having achieved a good credit rating. Debt is something to be tolerated in certain situations and only for defined periods of time under rigid guidelines.

Dealing with debt is like owning a python. You have to know what you're doing, always exercising a great deal of caution because if you slack off and lose control, it could strangle you to death.

When you incur debt, you make a rather arrogant presumption on the future. In effect, you're saying that you don't have the money to buy that thing that you want now—this could be anything from a house to a pair of shoes—but you assume you will have the money in the future to make payments. You presume that you will have a job, that you will have your health so you can perform your job. You presume that you will love whatever it is you went into debt to acquire as much as you love it now—and that it will not become obsolete or used up for as long as the debt remains—so that making the payments will not become drudgery. Acquiring a debt is simple compared to all that is required to carry and eventually pay off that debt. Simply making the promise to repay makes presumptions, and some of them quite arrogant, on the future.

Debt transfers future wealth to one's creditors. No matter how much you may want to build wealth for retirement or to pass on to your children, it won't be there if you stay in debt. Whatever you hope to have in the future, for yourself or others, already belongs to those who lent you the money to buy what you have today.

One estimate is that Baby Boomers (defined as those who were born between 1946 and 1964) stand to inherit $11.6 trillion, largely from their parents.[1] Those who have managed to land themselves in a deep pit of debt will experience the sadness I hear from so many readers—transferring what they hoped would become future wealth to their creditors to pay off a large accumulation of revolving debt.

Never forget that as hard as it is to make a living, it's a lot harder to earn money that you've already spent.

Debt promotes discontentment. Debt is often what happens when you're not satisfied with what you can afford to have right now. And once you start pursuing "more," you'll always be unhappy with what you have at the moment because, face it, there will always be something more out there that captures your attention. It's easy to use debt as the antidote for feelings of dissatisfaction and discontentment. Then it becomes akin to drinking a glass of salty water. It makes you thirsty so you want to drink more, and the more you drink the thirstier you become.

Debt limits your options. This is true of any type of debt, even a secured home mortgage. Debt is like a lead balloon that holds you down in one spot. You have a legal obligation and no choice but to keep earning whatever you can to pay it off—even if the things that incurred the debt were wants or items long since consumed. Because you turned them into debt, the debt payment has become a "need" or essential expense. You have no flexibility to follow other dreams or any other call on your life, no matter how noble or godly. You have to pay your debts first.

The financial obligation incurred by debt can keep you chained to a job you dislike or living in a home that no longer meets your needs if due to market conditions you are unable to sell that home to pay off the debt. Debt can limit your options when it comes to a future spouse when you come chained to a load of debt your beloved simply cannot accept.

It can remove options for where your kids will go to school or whether you can afford to have kids at all.

I could go on and on, but I think you get my point regarding how options can disappear in the face of debt.

Debt is expensive. No matter how you look at it, when you opt to go into debt to pay for a home, car, or any other thing you can think of—you will pay dearly for that dubious privilege.

Example: take a $200,000 home on which you have a $160,000 mortgage payable at 5 percent interest over 30 years. Your monthly principal and interest payments will be $859. Here's what many people don't think about: $859 x 360 = $309,240. Add the $40,000 down payment and you will discover that your $200,000 home really cost $349,240. And that's at a fairly low rate of interest. How about a $1,500 engagement ring paid with a credit card at 22.99 percent interest under typical terms where the monthly payment is 4 percent of the outstanding balance? It will take 101 months (almost 9 years) and $1,175 of interest to pay it off, for a total cost of $2,675.

If you are ever tempted to buy something because it is such a bargain that you cannot afford not to buy it, but you don't have the money so you must use credit, do this before you make your final decision: double the sale price. Is it still such a great bargain? Probably not, but that's what it's going to cost if you opt to pay for it over a long period of time.

A Safety Net Reduces Trouble

While it is always better to not have debt, at times it is unavoidable. So just like living with a python, you become masterful at putting safety measures in place. The stronger your safety nets, the less likely it is that you will be harmed by the debt.

When I refer to "safety nets," I mean the guidelines and precautionary measures that are part of Rule 7. Those who throw caution to the wind, venturing into the world of consumer debt without safety nets in place (I include myself in those I am about to call foolish), have lots of scars to show for their foolishness. And it is not only the horrendous amounts of wasted money but also the myriad lost opportunities.

Here's the bottom line: debt is not a good thing, and it is to be avoided whenever possible. When it cannot be avoided, debt should be entered into advisedly, with tremendous caution and a strong system of safety nets in place.

Three Categories of Debt

All debt falls into one of three categories: reasonable, toxic, and neutral.

Reasonable, or good debt, is the result of borrowing money to buy something that has a high likelihood of increasing in value, and in so doing will increase your net worth. Buying a home with a low-risk mortgage would be an example of reasonable debt because as the debt is repaid and the home appreciates in value, your net worth will increase proportionately. That is financially reasonable, without imposing an unreasonable financial risk for you, the borrower. A reasonably small amount of student loan debt can also come under the umbrella of good or reasonable debt, provided it meets certain criteria as described on the following page, because you have a reasonable likelihood of getting a better-paying job after you graduate than you would've without the education.

Toxic debt is exactly as the name implies: dangerous and financially life threatening. Toxic debt includes credit card debt, payday loans, and other high- or variable-rate borrowing. Toxic debt is deadly and should be avoided entirely. Toxic debt is not secured by collateral, and the interest rates are typically so huge they could choke a horse. If you have toxic debt, it needs to be paid off quickly (see chapter 13) and then avoided in the future by every means possible. I cannot state this too strongly: toxic debt is hazardous to your wealth.

Neutral debt includes all other borrowing that is neither good because it's not going to increase wealth in any way, nor bad because it's not exactly toxic.

With these definitions in mind let's look at general guidelines for Rule 7 borrowing, followed by specifics for the different types of borrowing.

Safe Borrowing Guidelines

The following guidelines apply to all forms of borrowing—all forms of debt.

1. Borrow the least you can get by with to achieve your intended result, not the most that the lender will approve. Never let a lender determine how much you should borrow. Mortgage lenders will try to nudge you into the "most house you can qualify for," not the house you can afford.

2. Repay debt quickly, rather than stretching it out as far as possible. Opt for the largest payment you can handle, not the smallest the lender will approve.

Auto lenders will try to steer you into a long-term loan of 60 to 72 months, pointing out that your payment will be smaller. This is great for them because dragging it out over a longer period of time with smaller monthly payments means you'll be paying a lot more interest over the term of the loan. That adds up to a big payout for the lender, but it's a lousy deal for you.

3. Have an escape plan. You need to have a plan in mind to pay off the debt early in the event life takes an unexpected turn, either by selling the collateral or paying the debt with other resources or assets.

Home Mortgage Debt

For a home mortgage to be a debt you know that you can repay, the principal owing should never be more than 80 percent of the home's market value with a monthly payment that is no more than 25 percent of the borrower's net income. Example: if the purchase price of the home is $250,000, you should borrow no more than $200,000 ($250,000 x 80% = $200,000). This creates a comfortable margin that will give you reasonable certainty that you can repay that loan either through the repayment schedule or by selling the property at market value and using the difference between the selling price (market value) and the balance to pay off the outstanding mortgage.

With the real estate housing crash and the Great Recession so fresh in our memories, it's important that we talk about this matter of "underwater" mortgages, which means that for whatever reason, a borrower ends up owing more than the property is worth. At that point, the debt becomes toxic if there is not sufficient collateral to repay the loan upon the borrower's whim. This is a critical point that every homeowner needs to anticipate by knowing with certainty where the market value of the home is in relationship to the amount owed.

The way to avoid falling into this kind of situation is to always maintain a healthy margin between the amount you owe and the home's market value. By stringently adhering to the criteria that your outstanding mortgage principal balance should never be more than 80 percent of the home's current market value, you'll be in a safe position.

Each month as you make your mortgage payment you will increase the gap between the home's value and what you owe, so that even if the market value fluctuates down you're in a good position to keep your head above water, so to speak. Soon you'll owe 75 percent, then 70, and then you will owe nothing and enjoy 100 percent equity. You will own that house free and clear, which is the intended purpose of having a mortgage in the first place.

A closer look at most "underwater" mortgage situations of the past few years would most likely reveal mortgages that were already close to, if not greater than, the home's market value. Borrowers were able to buy homes with nothing down (100 percent loans), and in some cases lenders, for a fee, would lend more than the home's market value, assuming that the value would appreciate and soon catch up.

Home Equity Loans

A home equity loan, curiously known in the industry as HEL, is typically a second mortgage that allows the homeowner access to the equity (that margin between what is owed and what the property is worth). Equity is the borrower's asset—and a precious asset at that.

Theoretically a HEL is a secured or safe debt because it is collateralized by the home's market value. Upon the borrower's desire to repay the debt, the home can be sold to satisfy both the first mortgage and the HEL, also known as a second mortgage. Please do not miss the operative word "theoretically."

A HEL can be very risky because it can so easily lead to toxic debt. There are five ways the toxic factor can sneak into an otherwise intelligent, safe mortgage situation.

1. If you borrow against your equity to clean up your credit card debt and then run up your credit cards all over again (a very common occurrence, by the way, with people who take the route of cashing in home equity to pay off toxic credit card debt), that leaves you with twice the debt—the HEL and the credit cards. Not smart.

2. Some people treat a home equity loan as a permanent debt to be paid off when the house is sold. They might have felt a greater urgency to pay off the debts if they were in the form of credit card balances. The delay in paying off the HEL opens the door to the home's value dropping, thus making the total debt owed greater than the home's market value. This is what happened during the recent real estate market crash as millions of homeowners stripped their home equity by use of the HEL, treating their homes more like ATMs or giant piggy banks, rather than appreciating assets. The US economy is paying dearly for such foolishness.

3. The convenience of having your home's equity available at your fingertips can be a formidable temptation. Knowing the money is readily available, you are more likely to fritter it away on something like a well-deserved family vacation instead of saving the money first as you might have if you did not have such easy access to your precious equity.

4. If you are unable to keep current on both of your mortgages (the underlying first mortgage as well as the HEL), either of the lenders can foreclose.

5. Sometimes the home equity loan and first mortgage together actually exceed the current market value of the property. Shockingly, some lenders are still willing to finance a home for more than it is worth—even as much as 125 percent of the property's value, which begs the question: didn't we learn anything from the housing bubble burst in 2006 that resulted in prices falling further than they did in the Great Depression?[2] And didn't lawmakers quickly enact laws to prevent such a thing from happening again in the future? While many mortgage lenders have become more cautious, there are no laws that prevent this kind of predatory lending. There are plenty of lenders still willing to make 125-percent HELs that put the borrower in a tenuous position where the monthly payments are severe, but selling the property ceases to be a way out because more is owed than it would bring at sale.

Even taking into consideration the fact that the interest on the home equity loan may be deductible from your taxable income, the risks involved with this potentially toxic debt can be weighty.

The equity in your home is an appreciating asset, for many people their only appreciating asset. If you leave it alone, it will grow as the property becomes more valuable and as you pay down the first mortgage. That contributes to the safety factor of your home's mortgage. To muddy those waters with an HEL opens the door to toxic debt.

Student Debt

Student loan debt best falls into the "neutral" category, as we categorize debt. And it walks a very fine line. Unsecured student loan debt can easily tumble off into the pit of toxic debt.

You will recall from chapter 1 that the total student loan debt outstanding in the US has grown to $850 billion, which exceeds the outstanding credit card debt, now standing at $828 billion. That's huge and not a matter to be taken lightly. Untold millions of adults are drowning in student debt, which has become a worse problem for them than their credit card debt. Student debt, unlike credit card debt, cannot be discharged through bankruptcy. There is a fine line between neutral and toxic when it comes to student debt, and is something you need to consider very carefully before taking an educational debt plunge.

The biggest issue for me when it comes to borrowing money to pay for college is this matter of reserves. Where's the money held in reserve to pay off the student loan debt? Theoretically that reserve is held in your ability to earn that money quickly upon completing school and landing a job in an industry that will welcome you and your degree. Something that would have been closed to you without that education. That's the theory.

Now let's talk reality. With 85 percent of college graduates returning home to live with their parents upon graduation because they cannot find a job,[3] I need to give a very strong warning when it comes to racking up student debt. Student debt always comes with a high level of risk due to the lack of collateral, but never higher than in this season of tremendous economic challenge facing the US.

First and foremost, if you are planning to get student loans, choose a school and major where there's a demonstrated track record of return on investment. Law, medicine, nursing, and engineering are considered fairly safe bets as there are jobs in those fields.

Of course, if you can fund your education without any loans through scholarships, grants, and paying as you go, that will be the most ideal. As a general rule, public state colleges and universities and community colleges are cheaper than private institutions, which reduces your financial risk. If you feel that you absolutely must go the student loan route, you will have to create your own limits on how much you will borrow. The school will want to be very generous by offering everything for which you can qualify. Do not see this as some kind of prophecy that you will actually be able to make the repayments on all of the money you could be allowed to borrow.

To keep your student loan under the umbrella of "reasonable debt," your total student debt (all four years) should not exceed the average first year entry level salary in the industry for which you are preparing. Check the "Student Loans Occupation Handbook" online at http://www.bls.gov/oco

/home.htm/ to get an idea what your first-year salary might be. It is reasonable that you could repay your entire student debt within the first three years of your working career. That should be your goal.

While federal guidelines do not require borrowers to make any payments on their student loans until after they leave school, do not take that option. Instead, start making the small monthly interest payments as soon as you take the loan. This will preclude a negative amortization situation where the unpaid interest each month is added back into the loan as additional principal so that by the time you get around to paying off your loans (once you are out of school) you owe far more than you borrowed.

Let me give you an example. Let's say that you borrow $5,000 in September of your first semester as a freshman, at an interest rate of 6.9 percent. Because of the terms of a student loan, you are not required to make payments until you leave school. But that doesn't mean the interest is not owed during those years. In this example, the first month's interest calculated at 6.9 percent APR (annual percentage rate) on $5,000 is $28.75 ($5,000 x .069 = $345 ÷ 12 = $28.75). If you do not pay that amount, in October your principal owing will be $5,028.75. You now owe more than you borrowed because the interest you did not pay became part of the principal. In November you will owe interest on the $5,028.75. This is called negative amortization. In November you will be charged 6.9 percent APR on $5,028.75, which is $28.91. If you do not pay it, it becomes part of the principal, and your debt will grow to $5,057.66. If you wait for four years and six months to start paying this loan, just imagine how much $5,000 will have become.

A better idea would be to pay $28.75 every month, while you are in school. When you finish school you will owe the original $5,000.

After you're out of school for six months, you must begin to make monthly payments on your accumulated student debt (if you have been making at least the interest payments all along, you will owe far less than if you have been avoiding that). Do not give in to temptation to put your loans into forbearance or deferment. That only pushes the pain of payment farther into the future, while the unpaid interest keeps piling up. Put yourself onto a fast repayment track to get the debts paid off as quickly as possible.

Credit Card Debt

Credit card debt is flat-out toxic. If you cannot pay the entire balance every month before the due date, so that you are never paying interest, stop using the accounts. Give the cards to a trusted friend or relative who will hide them for you. It's that serious!

If you are carrying toxic credit card debt now, determine that you will pay it off quickly (in chapter 13 I will show you how to do this quickly and effectively). There are few things you can do that will burn a hole through your discretionary income faster than paying double-digit interest each month for stuff you bought that you probably don't even have any longer.

I want to show you just how toxic credit card debt can be. Let's say that you are carrying a credit card revolving balance of $3,500, at an interest rate of 29.99 percent, and your minimum monthly payment is 4 percent of the outstanding balance. Even if you stop adding any new purchases to that account, it will take you 188 months (that's 15.6 years!) to be rid of that debt. In that time, you will pay $5,429 in interest. Another way to look at it, $3,500 grows to $8,929 by the time you pay it off. That is the true cost of toxic credit card debt.

As horrific as the foregoing example is, it's too kind for this reason: the typical person who carries this kind of credit card debt is not likely to go for 15.6 years without adding a single purchase. During that time, something will come up and the cardholder will slip just one more meal, another pair of shoes, or even a well-deserved vacation onto that account, turning it into a lifetime of toxicity.

Credit cards can be seductive with all of the rebates, cash back, and mileage points. The industry has done a great job at making us believe that carrying some toxic debt is not a problem. But it is. And it is very foolish to carry debt because you wanted to get the miles. Or to buy something on credit to get 2 percent cash back. It makes absolutely no financial sense to pay 29.99 percent on an item you can afford to buy outright because you wanted to get 2 percent cash back on the purchase price.

It takes financial intelligence and personal discipline to keep a credit card account active (see chapter 9) without allowing it to become a toxic situation. But millions of people do, and so can you. It requires discipline and a full understanding of how credit card accounts operate.

Automobile Debt

The only way to borrow safely to finance a car is to make sure its market value is always greater than the outstanding loan principal. Because cars depreciate, you need to save ahead for a healthy down payment, making sure you are borrowing the least, not the most, the lender will approve. Once your loan is in place, make it a race to get the car paid off faster than it is losing market value. The difference between what you owe on the car and the amount you could sell it for tomorrow afternoon is called "equity." You want to build equity faster than you are losing value due to depreciation. Once you reach 100 percent equity, you owe nothing and that car is fully paid.

Here are guidelines to make sure your car loan does not turn toxic. Keep the payments to 36 months or less. If you stretch it out longer, you will pay far too much interest and you run the risk of paying for car repairs on a car for which you're still making payments.

A car loan can contain elements of reasonable borrowing provided you make a large down payment, select a model that historically retains a high resale value, and pay it off in three years.

An automobile loan is a secured debt, which means that the car itself holds the reserves necessary to repay that loan. In theory you should be able to sell the car at any time to pay the debt. But here is the challenge to that situation: cars do not appreciate. Every day it loses value. Unless you are paying the loan faster than the car is depreciating, the debt can turn toxic.

Scripture on Debt

Given my history with credit and debt, I was surprised when I dug into the Bible to see what God has to say about borrowing money and going into debt. I expected to find the word "debt" synonymous with living a sinful lifestyle. Here's a quick overview of what I learned.

Debt is not forbidden or condemned, although God discourages it by giving us countless warnings against getting into debt.[4] Those in debt are warned to get out as fast as possible.[5] Those who do not pay their debts are cursed: "The wicked borrow and do not pay, but the righteous give generously."[6]

Debt is characterized as bondage: "The rich rule over the poor, and the borrower is servant to the lender."[7] I sure know what it feels like, and it doesn't feel good.

Lending money, on the other hand, is encouraged and seen as a good thing. God blesses those who have enough and are willing to lend to others.[8] It occurred to me that if, as I had assumed, borrowing money was evil, that would make those who lend accomplices, and that is not the case.

Borrowing money is not wrong, but it should be done advisedly and with tremendous caution. Debt of any kind should be seen as a short-term situation that always has an accompanying aggressive payment plan.

Debt should never be seen as ideal, but rather as a reasonable means to an end. Being debt free is ideal, and the goal for which you should be reaching with all the determination and strength you have.

11 Getting It All Together

Knowledge is the difference between really living and just existing. Existing is instinctual; living is the exercise of certain learned skills, attitudes, and abilities that you have acquired and honed to a sharp and focused edge.

—Phillip C. McGraw ("Dr. Phil")

I don't know the circumstance of your life, but I am going to make a few assumptions. Something prompted you to pick up this book, quite possibly a desire to improve or change the way you handle your money. Good. You're still here, which means you know what the 7 Rules are. Even better. That tells me that you are motivated to apply this information to your life.

Any kind of life change should be approached as a challenge that calls for endurance and a survivor's spirit. Again, I don't know the circumstances of your financial life, but I do know something about what it takes to make permanent life changes. It is hard work. If it were easy, no one would be in debt, no one would struggle to spend less than they earn, and the world would be a much different place.

There is no elevator to the top when it comes to changing the way you manage money. It's one step at a time. And if you are in a difficult financial situation, it's going to be uphill for a while.

Endurance and Survival

I am totally fascinated by stories and documentaries that depict the remarkable will to endure and survive that we find in the animal kingdom.

Take the emperor penguins of Antarctica. Every year in autumn, they leave their cozy ocean habitat and take a journey that spans hundreds of miles, walking across a frozen continent to their inland breeding grounds. In a tortuous march that takes many months, these birds brave unspeakably brutal conditions to bring new life into the world.

I am no less amazed when I read accounts of pets who by some set of circumstances become separated from their human families. Many years and thousands of miles later, Fido or Fluffy turns up on the front porch. How do animals know the way, and how do they find the stamina and courage to survive in the face of such insurmountable obstacles?

There's no doubt that many animals, fish and fowl alike, are endowed with supernatural survival skills. But they've got nothing on you.

You, too, have been created with a tremendous capacity for endurance and survival. But with one important addition: you can think. You have a human brain. You have the capacity to learn, reason, and make decisions. More than that, you can choose your thoughts. And by virtue of that, you have the power to change your life.

Knowledge or Entertainment?

You have just spent the better part of this book learning 7 essential rules for managing money. You've added to your knowledge bank. But so what?

Don't get me wrong. Knowledge is a wonderful thing and I am thrilled that I might have imparted something of importance to you. But until what we learn moves us to action, it's nothing more than entertainment. If you do not apply these rules to your life, you've wasted your time and money. And ended up with another book gathering dust on your bookshelf.

Please don't let that happen. Don't stop with the knowledge. Determine right now that you will turn these rules into tools; that you will move from knowledge to action.

Because you are still with me in chapter 11, you know the 7 Rules. The next question is: what will you do with them?

By applying each of the 7 Rules to your life by setting specific goals, you will activate them in your life.

7 Rules, 7 Tools

If there's a lesson I've learned on my journey from debt to solvency it's this: goals not written are but a dream. A dream is great, but it's no financial plan. Dreams are flighty, fickle, and forgettable.

For your dreams to become reality, they have to become written goals. Write down your goals, make plans to achieve them, and then work on those plans every single day. This is where your human brain is going to come in handy because of what I just mentioned: you have the capacity to choose your thoughts.

You can choose to think about your goals every day or you can choose not to. Either is a clear-cut choice. When it comes to thoughts there is no neutral default point. Not thinking about your financial situation and not doing everything you can to change the course of your financial life is a conscious choice. Not a good one, in my opinion, but a choice nonetheless.

Write, Commit, Become Accountable

A Dominican University study offers enlightening data on the value of writing goals, as opposed to just thinking about them.[1] Participants in the scientific study were divided between those who wrote their goals, those who simply thought about them, and those who became accountable to a supportive friend for their progress.

The results bear out what I know to be true in my life: those participants who wrote their goals accomplished significantly more than those who did not write their goals. And those who wrote their goals and became accountable by sending weekly progress reports to a trusted friend accomplished the most.

Once you write a goal, no matter how simple it is, it takes on power of its own. You have something specific on which to focus. Your thoughts point to it like a laser beam, which leads to another powerful benefit of your human brain: you become what you think about most of the time.

148

By deciding what you want to achieve, writing it down, and then choosing to focus on it, you begin to move toward it. It's an automatic response and one you can count on.

Here's a nonfinancial-type goal that we'll use as an example. Let's say that you have decided to begin eating more healthfully. Your doctor has suggested you should do this and you've read studies on the health benefits of eating organic foods and avoiding preservatives. You're convinced that it's time to make a change. You purge the pantry, create healthy menus, and load up on the foods you are determined to eat from now on. And you create a simple journal on your computer.

First entry:

> My Healthy Eating Goal. In 30 days I will drop 5 pounds by eating more healthfully. To do this I will cut out all soda, include 5 servings of fresh fruits and vegetables in my diet each day, and eliminate all refined sugar.

That is a reachable goal because it is clear, written, and specific. Its progress is measurable at any time by stepping on the scale.

Last, you make a conscious effort to focus on this goal by pledging to read it at least once daily and developing any thoughts you have or changes you need to make.

If your goal is written, reasonable, and measurable—and you choose to focus on it most of the time—I will make a bold prediction: you will achieve it.

Let's say you are tempted to duck into the ice cream shop. Go ahead, but just be prepared for the loud megaphones that will go off in your head, pushing your goal right into your face, making you rethink what you're about to do.

When you find yourself in a restaurant, menu in hand, about to order the deep fried apple pie, loud reminders will go off between your ears.

When you need to buy groceries, you'll be duly prompted which aisles to visit. And if you swerve down the candy aisle and feel the need to stop, it won't be guilt tapping on your shoulder. It's your natural capacity to achieve goals that will suggest you should just keep going.

Setting goals, working toward them every day, and finally reaching them is the way to change your financial future. Your goals need not be huge. In fact, setting smaller goals makes sense. With shorter benchmarks, you'll reach your goals more quickly, providing the boost you'll need to set a new goal, or 12, until finally you've changed your life.

One Step at a Time

I love to knit. That is not to say that I am a fast knitter or even that good at it. It's not the finished product that I find so enjoyable. It's the process, the way it works. It's the gentle rhythm, the pulling of one loop of yarn through another, over and over.

Curiously, knitting has only two stitches: knit and purl. That's true for me and even the most advanced knitter on the face of the earth. Just two stitches. No matter if I go fast or slow, how intricate or ordinary the pattern, I can make only one stitch at a time and one stitch makes absolutely no visual difference whatsoever. That's just the way it is with knitting.

Now and then I come to the last stitch, bind it off, and surprise even myself by what I've created. How did that happen?

It's remarkable that just one stitch at a time can bring such pleasing results.

As you begin to make changes in the ways you manage your money and take control of your future, don't set yourself up for failure by making giant goals that are unreasonable and therefore unreachable.

The Rule Team

You could approach your overall money management plan one rule at a time, opting to master it, then move on to the next rule. But as I said earlier in the book, I do not recommend that. The 7 Rules work together. They are part of one whole. So if you choose to work on one rule at a time, placing the others in abeyance, things will fall out of balance. You could be setting yourself up for frustration.

A much better option, in my opinion, is to begin applying all of the rules to your life now.

Here are some examples for 7 Rules goals that fit the criteria that a goal needs to be written, reasonable, and measurable.

Rule 1: Spend Less Than You Earn

In the coming 30 days, I will widen the gap between my income and spending by cooking at home and limiting restaurant meals to once a month.

Rule 2: Save for the Future

I will set up an automatic deposit to move $200 from each of my two monthly paychecks into my online savings account, and will continue this until the account reaches $25,000.

Rule 3: Give Some Away

I will take $50 from each of my two monthly paychecks and place it in my Giving Account. I will give this money to meet others' needs as I see those needs in my daily course of life. My intention is to bring this account down to $0 at least once every 60 days.

Rule 4: Anticipate Irregular Expenses

I will create a list of irregular expenses, then direct one-twelfth of the total into my special reserve account each month. I will continue to do this until I have accumulated enough to pay these expenses one year in advance.

Rule 5: Tell Your Money Where to Go

I will take control of where my money goes by creating a written Spending Plan that incorporates Rule 2 Saving, Rule 3 Giving, Rule 4 Reserves plus all of my regular expenses. Then I will track my spending throughout the month to measure it against my Spending Plan.

Rule 6: Manage Your Credit Rating

I will order at least one of my credit reports from Annual CreditReport.com within the next 30 days, review it thoroughly, disputing any errors I find and following up to make sure my credit report contains only factual information.

Rule 7: Borrow Only What You Know You Can Repay

I will cease all use of credit cards while aggressively paying down my toxic credit card debt using (shameless plug alert) Mary Hunt's Rapid Debt-Repayment Calculator and Manager at DebtProofLiving.com, a place I am going to learn more about in chapter 15.

12 The Irregular Income Challenge

Being self-employed is sometimes like walking on a treadmill.

—Andy Winn

If you are or ever have been self-employed or in a sales position where you are paid by commission, you might recognize the term "mystery means." That is the condition of never knowing from one month to the next what your income will be, if at all.

I have discovered over the years that this condition of irregular income is one that keeps many people stuck in debt and unable to effectively manage their personal finances with any hope of getting ahead.

Overview

If you are a freelancer, a consultant, or work in sales, the arts, or some other form of self-employment and don't know when or how much you'll be paid from month to month, you live on a kind of financial roller coaster. You may have dismissed

155

a couple of the 7 Rules as not applicable to your situation because, "If I don't know how much is coming in any given month, how can I plan for how I will spend it?"

The majority of those who fall into the irregular income category live in constant uncertainty. Some months there is absolutely no income and then a deal closes or a big account comes through with a good-sized check. It is easy to forget the lean months you just survived, or to recognize that there may be many more ahead.

I feel your pain, and I completely understand what you are going through. My husband and I have been self-employed for many years so this irregular income situation is not foreign to me. And I believe I have a plan for you that will help you take the peaks and valleys out of your income stream and put you into a perfect position to apply the 7 Rules to your life.

To qualify as one who is self-employed for our purposes here, you do not have to own a business. I consider self-employed anyone who attempts to earn a living as an entrepreneur, small business owner, freelancer, distributor, consultant, entertainer, artist, or commission sales—basically, anyone who cannot predict with certainty the amount of his or her next paycheck, I will refer to herein as "self-employed."

Two Parties

In any employment situation there are two parties: employer and employee. As a self-employed person you are both. You have "hired" yourself so now you must supervise, manage, and pay yourself too. You must learn to wear two different hats: one that reads You the Employer, the other You the

Employee. You cannot wear them at the same time because employers and employees think and operate differently. You must also learn how and when to switch hats.

Wanda, Wilson, and Widgets

Let's say your friend Wanda works for Mr. Wilson, owner of Widget World, Inc. Her salary is $40,000 a year, paid monthly.

The widget business is seasonal. Mr. Wilson sells far more widgets in the winter than the summer months. Wanda is a diligent employee, and while she knows the seasonality of widgets, it doesn't concern her. That's Mr. Wilson's business. She has a job to do, she does it well, and she collects her paycheck on the first day of every month, month after month after month.

Because Wanda has a "real job" she can predict her paychecks and is confident that even during her employer's slow months, she will still get paid.

So how does Mr. Wilson run this business and keep everything together when he really doesn't know from one month to the next how much money his widget business will generate? I'm sure you're way ahead of me here, but I'll tell you anyway: Mr. Wilson is careful to build up reserves. He does not spend all of the company's income during the good months, so he has cash available in the slow months to keep paying Wanda her monthly salary and his other business expenses too.

You, You, and Your Business

As a self-employed person, you have to be both Mr. Wilson and Wanda. You must do double duty. You work for yourself so you have to wear both hats. How foolish it would be for You the Employee to demand all of the money that You the Employer bring into the business each month. This is why the two of you need to sit down and negotiate a fixed salary that You the Employer can afford to pay and You the Employee can afford to live on.

THE FIRST STEP

As a self-employed person you must determine what is the least amount of money you must have every month to live, not the most you can possibly wrangle out of You the Employer.

If you created your Rule 5 Spending Plan, you know how much that is. It's a bottom-line number that includes Rule 2 Saving, Rule 3 Giving, Rule 4 Reserves Payment, your rent or mortgage payment, transportation, insurance, food, and so on. Let's say you determine that you cannot live on less than $3,000 a month. That is the least that You the Employee must receive each month if you are going to work here.

CAN YOU AFFORD YOU?

You the Employer must determine if your business can reasonably commit to hiring a $3,000-a-month salaried employee. Let's assume that you can, so you offer You the Employee a job.

SEPARATE FUNDS

No matter how small or part-time your self-employment situation is, the secret to your success will be in maintaining a separate checking account for your business. You should never deposit personal funds into it or pay for personal expenses from it.

Two Scenarios

Scenario #1: Let's say that you are a self-employed freelance writer. You receive royalty checks from your publisher every quarter, you write for several magazines and receive checks from them each month, and you do copyediting for a publishing company on an as-needed basis. You get checks at random times for all of these different writing jobs, contracts, and assignments, and they come payable to you as an individual. They look like paychecks.

Your husband gets paid each Friday, so you hold any checks you've received during the week until then and make one deposit to your personal household account because he is not self-employed. But your checks from your freelance writing, even the pathetically small ones, are technically business income, not personal funds.

Mr. Wilson does not allow Wanda to take checks made payable to Widget Word, Inc., and deposit them into her personal checking account. That would be ridiculous. And you should not be paying yourself with checks you receive in payment of work you do (even if they are made out to you personally).

You must recognize the difference between business and personal income if you expect to make a success of self-employment. You must have a separate checking account into which you deposit business income and from which you pay yourself a salary.

Scenario #2: In this situation, let's say you are employed as a commissioned salesperson. Your company issues you "paychecks" but only as you earn a commission. They withhold taxes just as they do for their salaried employees.

You start off the year with a bang by generating a $10,000 commission check. You deposit it into your regular household account. In February you receive nothing even though you've worked hard. Nothing again in March.

In April you receive four checks for $1,550, $1,200, $4,000, and $850, all of which go straight into your personal checking account and not a moment too soon. That's $17,600 for four months. Because all of your commissions come from your employer, you think of them as paychecks.

The problem is, in January you had to play catch-up on all of the holiday bills that you couldn't pay because December had been a "dry" month. You had to cover late fees, overdraft fees, plus bring all of your utility bills current. And there were all of those great after-Christmas sales. You felt as if you had extra money because you knew about that big commission check coming in January, so you splurged.

Along comes February and March with no income. Your personal checking account is depleted even though you are working hard and closing a few deals. You call the credit cards into action, and it's desperation time again until April. The four checks you get in April ($7,600) are barely enough to catch you up. You enter May with a big fat $0 in the bank.

The Way It Should Work

This is how the self-employment situation of Scenario #2 should be handled.

First, even though you are an employee of a company that pays you by commissions, you need to open a checking account that you designate to be your "business account." This is separate from your personal household bank account.

The January $10,000 check gets deposited into your business checking account. You guard this account from You the Employee as any good business owner would. Employees should not have direct access to business funds. Even if there are household needs and expenses, you do not use a dime of that $10,000 to pay for them directly.

On January 15, your "payday," you write out a paycheck for $3,000, regardless of the balance in the business checking account. You deposit this into your personal checking account. This is difficult because you really could use some more money to get through January, and there is money sitting there in your business account. But You the Employee cannot expect a raise every month, in the same way Wanda does not expect one from Mr. Wilson even when she could use more money and knows he has plenty.

You get $3,000 on payday and that's it until next payday.

On February 15, you write yourself another $3,000 paycheck from the business account even though you've had no business income this month.

On March 15, you write yourself a $3,000 paycheck. On April 15 you deposit the $7,600 commission checks into your business account and write yourself a $3,000 paycheck. Your business account is never depleted.

Now you know the secret for how to turn mystery means into a predictable and regular paycheck. This, too, is called money management.

Give Yourself a Raise

In time, as things continue to go well and you're able to build sufficient reserves, You the Employer might decide to negotiate a raise for your favorite employee. But don't be too hasty.

Weigh the pros and cons. Consider the position of the prudent employer against the needs of the employee. Employers cannot afford to deal from emotion. They must consider the best interests of both the company and the employee.

The wise employer knows that if the company goes under that will be infinitely worse for the employee than a pathetically small raise.

Successfully Self-Employed

As a self-employed person, your biggest challenge will be the temptation to live it up when a big check comes in. Worse, you will be tempted to multiply your best month by 12 and convince yourself that is your annual income. Let go of that. The only way that you can establish your annual income is by looking at your past years' tax returns and taking an average. That's reality.

Your success as a self-employed person lies in your ability to discipline yourself to be a fair yet strict employer and at the same time a grateful, restrained, and patient employee. You the Employee must become ultra-conservative and fanatically frugal even when you have seasons of financial success. You need all the financial reserves you can amass in order to move yourself away from the edge and never knowing for sure how much you'll be making next month.

If your business is unable to pay You the Employee a living wage (in money, not credit), it's time to decide if you have a viable business or if this is a hobby that might one day be a business. A business's ability to pay its employees and expenses is what makes it viable.

If you determine that you have a hobby but you need a paycheck, go to work for someone who can afford to pay you. When your hobby becomes a viable business, you'll be able to offer yourself a real job.

Recap

You level out the extremes of the self-employed roller-coaster ride when you:

1. Put yourself on a strict salary.
2. Accept from your "employer" the very least you can live on, not the most.
3. Call into action every frugal tactic possible.
4. Underestimate the income the business will produce.
5. Overestimate the expenses. Double them and you'll probably get it right.

13 Drowning in Debt

Today, there are three kinds of people: the have's, the have-not's, and the have-not-paid-for-what-they-have's.

—Earl Wilson

I know something about paying off toxic debt. Years ago my husband and I paid off more than $100,000 of wicked, toxic debt. We didn't have a particular plan, counsel, or guidance in how to go about doing it. We just kept working at it, and 13 years later we reached our goal of $0 debt.

Yes, it is remarkable and I am proud that we did. But the way that we did it wasn't smart. It cost way more than it should have in interest alone. The problem is we spread it out far too long—13 years! If I'd known then what I know now, we could have been out of debt in five years by applying a different method of paying it, and we could have kept a lot of money we ended up paying out in interest.

There is not a single "right" method for repaying toxic debt. Recently, I was assigned to write a feature story for a popular magazine. I interviewed five women who had paid back significant sums of toxic debt. Each one used a different method.

One sold everything of value that she owned and used the proceeds to pay her debt.

Another introduced an extreme austerity program to her family of eight and laid down the law. They didn't eat out for two years. They locked up the clothes dryer, hanging the clothes inside on clothes lines. They stopped watering the lawn and lowered their water bill. Her list of extreme measures was certainly attention-getting.

Another of my interviewees sold her home to pay her debt then rented a home one-third the size.

As I pondered these real-life stories, it dawned on me that while each woman used a different method, all of them reached their goal. They were all debt free.

From that I concluded that any method to pay off toxic debt will work. Eventually. The unknowns are the time it will take and how much additional interest you will pay by spreading it out too far. But still, the lesson was not lost on me: as long as you are going in the right direction, you are focused on your goal, and you choose to think about it most of the time, you will get there. You will succeed. Guaranteed.

One of the interviewees turned out to be a follower of my Debt-Proof Living family. Her method for getting free from her toxic debt was to follow my Rapid Debt-Repayment Plan® (RDRP). I was more than excited to hear her story.

She confirmed what I suspected: she paid back the debt in record time in a reasonable way that did not require her to sell the house or kill the grass. And she did it in less than three years.

Over a period of nearly 20 years I've had the wonderful privilege to lead thousands of people out of debt using the RDRP. Each time I get to speak with one of them it's so exciting, it is almost like experiencing that joy for the first time.

Many people, myself included, say getting out of toxic debt is like being released from prison. The sense of accomplishment is indescribable, but even that does not compare to the sense of financial relief that comes with the accomplishment.

RDRP Overview

In a nutshell, here's how the Rapid Debt-Repayment Plan works: you pay off your debt with the shortest term (usually that is your smallest debt) first and then use the extra money to prepay other loans. The RDRP's simple concept is what makes it so exciting. This method is likely the most pain free of any that I know of because it is based on your current minimum monthly payments. If you can keep up with your current minimum monthly payments, you can get out of debt and in record time.

The key to turning the concept into action is to follow five simple RDRP Rules (yes, more rules!) and to create a chart that you can hang on your refrigerator that shows in black and white your detailed payment schedule right down to the final $0. I will show you an example of this in a few pages.

RDRP Basics

The RDRP creates a custom plan to pay off all your unsecured, toxic debt that uses your current minimum monthly payments. This is really important so let me say this again. Your plan to pay off your debts will use the same small monthly payments that you made this month on your credit card accounts. You will not need to add any additional funds to the amounts you are paying right now. This is the beauty of this plan: it takes the very least amount you are required to pay this month, uses that figure to establish your base, and then turns it into your get-out-of-debt card.

This is a key point and one that many people miss when they assume that there's no way they can get out of debt because they cannot possibly pay more than the minimum payment.

You do not have a choice whether or not to pay your minimum monthly payments this month. And your RDRP is based on those minimum payments. Therefore, it is a plan you can and must put into effect immediately. It requires no new funding from you. It simply takes what you are already required to pay and turns it into a plan that will effectively get you out of debt, and in record time.

The Rapid Debt-Repayment Plan is designed for your unsecured debts. That does not mean the concept will not work for auto loans, home equity loans (HELs), and even mortgages. However, I want to caution you to not include your secured debts in your initial RDRP. The focus of the RDRP is ridding you of the most egregious of your debts, your toxic debts, which are your high-interest, unsecured consumer debts.

The Rapid Debt-Repayment Plan consists of five simple rules.

Rule 1. No new debt. This means you must immediately stop adding any new purchases to your credit cards. Period. No exceptions. You cannot put out a raging fire if you continue to pour gasoline on it. You cannot stop your bathtub from overflowing unless you turn off the tap. You cannot get out of debt unless you stop adding to it.

If you do not stop incurring new debt, no plan will ever work for you. The women I interviewed for the story had one thing in common: *they stopped adding to their debt mess!*

If you do not stop incurring new debt, you will go to your grave in perma-debt, which is a depressing thought but something you need to consider.

Rule 2. Add up your current minimum payments. Make a list of the payments you must make this month on your credit cards, store charge cards, installment loans, and personal loans. Include medical and dental payments—every unsecured debt for which you are currently responsible. This total amount is the amount you will pay toward your RDRP every month until you are debt free. Look at it. It is your new RDRP payment and it will not change from month to month. It's a new fixed monthly expense that will take the place of all of the smaller payments you scramble to pay to your credit card issuers each month.

Rule 3. Line up your debts from smallest to largest. Put your smallest debt on the top and then in order with the largest at the bottom. Do not arrange them according to the interest rate. The reason why you want the smallest debt at the top is that it will be paid off most quickly. You will need that emotional boost to keep you going. You won't believe how fantastic it feels to pay that first debt in full.

Rule 4. Pay the same amount every month. Do not pay attention to your creditors who will say you can pay less each month, which is what we call the "falling payment" method. For example, if your payment this month to your

Visa account is $43, that will be your monthly payment to that debt until it is paid in full even though Visa will accept less as your balance declines. If the total of your debt payments this month is say, $300, this Rule 4 requires that you pay that same amount every month until you are debt free. The RDRP will show you how to divvy up that $300 each month until you are free from the debt prison.

Rule 5. As one debt is paid, add its payment to the regular payment of the next debt in line. This is where the "rapid" kicks in because you are pre-paying your debts with payments far greater than required. But still your total monthly debt payment remains the same. This is the key to getting out of debt fast.

Emotional Payoff

If you are struggling with the idea of concentrating on the shortest debt first (not necessarily the one with the highest interest rate), understand that there's a good reason: you are going to need a big emotional payoff as quickly as possible. Reaching that first $0 is going to give you an emotional payoff like you never dreamed possible. You need a plan that works and one you will stick with. This is it. Believe me.

An Easier Way

Developing your RDRP by hand using a calculator is not impossible, but it is tedious. This is why we created the RDRP Calculator®, which is a member benefit of DebtProof Living.com. You simply input your current balances, interest

Rapid Debt-Repayment Plan®

These debts were arranged in order of the number of months left to pay them off.

First zero balance in just three months!

Now add that $25 to the next debt on the list until that charge is paid off.

Creditor	No. Mos.	Bal.	% Int	Payment Month																	
				1	2	3	4	5	6	7	8	9	10	11	12	13	14	15	16	17	18
Debt Store	3	71	20.9	25	25	23	0														
MasterCard	9	597	16.9	55	55	57	80	80	80	80	80	76	0								
Visa	11	478	18.9	40	40	40	40	40	40	40	40	44	120	46	0						
Dad	13	1500	00.0	100	100	100	100	100	100	100	100	100	100	174	220	116	0				
Orthodontist	17	1950	12.0	80	80	80	80	80	80	80	80	80	80	80	80	184	300	300	300	133	0
Totals		4596		300	300	300	300	300	300	300	300	300	300	300	300	300	300	300	300	133	0

The total of the minimum monthly payment in the first month was $300—as it will remain until all debts are paid off.

In month 12 Dad received his regular $100, plus the $120 that used to go to the department store, MasterCard and Visa, for a total of $220. He'll be completely paid off in month 13.

Debt-Free in 18 months!*

*This same scenario would take 96 months or 8 years (assuming you add no new debt) to repay using the method preferred by your credit card companies, which isn't surprising as they want you to be in debt forever. The rapid Debt-Repayment Plan® is a registered trademark of Mary Hunt's Debt-Proof Living and reprinted here with permission.

rates, and current payments. One click produces your custom RDRP showing the exact month you will be debt free. It also shows you how much you will save in the future if you begin saving your total payments once you are debt free. It is truly remarkable and will inspire you to get into a RDRP frame of mind . . . now!

Take a look at the RDRP example below. You see that by following the five simple RDRP rules, the entire debt is repaid in just 18 months. This same debt load paid back according to the creditor's plan would have taken more than 8 years, assuming you add no more new debt!

Don't Cancel Accounts

It will be tempting for you to cancel all of your toxic credit card accounts once you reach $0 balances on all of them. Don't give in to that temptation. As you know from Rule 6, your credit score is a financial tool that you will need to protect. Canceling multiple accounts all at once could cause considerable damage to your score. The reason, as you will recall, has to do with your "utilization rate." By canceling accounts, you reduce your total amount of available credit.

Of course I think you should be rewarded, not punished, for paying off a credit card and closing the account! But I don't write the rules, at least not those rules.

Reasonable Way to Close Accounts

If you have quite a few accounts that you would like to close, there is a way that you can do this that won't cause undue damage to your credit rating. Just make sure that the account has a $0 balance before you attempt to close it.

You do not want to close multiple credit card accounts at the same time. In fact, one or two a year is the rate at which you should do this. This is a slow enough rate that your credit score should escape any undue damage. You might see a few points come off, but the score should be restored after a short period of time.

But first, the facts. Banks, credit card companies, and retail credit granters are very keen on retaining their revolving or "open end" credit accounts (from the Latin root meaning there's no end to the amount of money we intend to squeeze from you during your lifetime. Or, we love you and we have a wonderful plan for your money.)

These companies paid dearly to bait, snag, and then reel you in. Since that time you've rewarded them handsomely. When they learn you're breaking up with them, they are not going to be happy. Reminder: it is not advisable to close an account until you have achieved $0 balance. To do otherwise invites an interest rate increase to the maximum allowed by law, and, by the way, in some states there is no such law.

Make the call. Find the toll-free number for customer service (on the back of the credit card itself, on the last statement, or on the company's website). Tell the customer service representative that you are requesting that they close your account. You'll get an argument, of course, but stick to your guns. You want to say, "Please close my account and report it as closed to the credit bureaus." Record the full name of this person and the date you made this request.

Send the letter. Immediately follow up with a letter that says the same thing. If you still have it, enclose the card, which you've cut into pieces. Send this letter by US Certified Mail with a request for a delivery and signature confirmation. This will cost you around $5, in addition to the regular postage, which as you know increases about every five minutes or so.

Follow up. About two weeks after that letter is delivered, call customer service again to confirm that your account has been closed. Assume it won't be closed (they're fighting you here, remember?). Repeat your verbal instructions. Close this account!

Verify. In about three months order a copy of your credit report. If the account shows "closed by request of customer" or some reasonable facsimile, you've achieved success. If not, go back to step one, make the call, and go through all the steps again.

Repeat as necessary. You could get full cooperation on your first call. Or it could take several rounds to permanently part company with this account.

Lesson to be learned. It's a lot easier to open than to close a credit card account. Even if you have all the current information like your account number, their customer service phone number, and address, it could cost you both in time, trouble, and postage. If not, your work will only multiply. Think about that the next time you're tempted to complete a new application.

14 Which Bills to Pay?

There's always something to be thankful for. If you can't pay your bills, you can be thankful you're not one of your creditors.

—Unknown

If you don't have enough money to pay all of your bills, which should you pay first and which ones can slide for a while? This is a question I get quite a bit, especially as more people are making employment transitions, while costs continue to soar.

Allowing bills to become delinquent is wrong, and certainly not something I am advocating. However, there are desperate situations when your available cash can be stretched only so far. That doesn't mean you are excused from payment, just that you need to know how to prioritize in a way that will cause the least amount of long-term damage and keep you in the best position to eventually catch up.

There are specific guidelines to follow when the bills you have due exceed the amount of money you have available to pay them. It is important that if you find yourself in this situation, you tenaciously follow this guideline: do not make payments on nonessential expenses when you have not paid essential ones, even if your nonessential creditors are breathing down your neck.

Essential Bills

An essential bill represents a serious obligation that if not paid could produce severe, even life-threatening consequences.

Once you've determined which debts are essential, prioritize them according to the severity of the consequences you will suffer for non-payment.

1. *Family necessities.* Usually this means basic food and unavoidable medical expenses including health insurance. While these expenses should be at the top of your priority list, they should also be kept to the absolute, bare bones minimum. You do not eat T-bone steaks three times a week or dine in fast food drive-thru lines when you are unable to pay the phone bill.
2. *Rent or mortgage.* Always assume that your landlord or mortgage lender will immediately proceed to evict or foreclose if you are late with a payment. Home equity loans and other consolidation loans secured by your home are essential debts and fall into this category. If you own your home, real estate taxes and insurance must also be paid unless they are included in the monthly payment.
3. *Utilities.* Next, you should pay the minimum required to keep essential utility services. You may not have to

pay the full amount of the bill, but the minimum necessary to avoid disconnection should be made, if at all possible.

4. *Car payments.* If a car is necessary to keep your job, making the loan or lease payment is the next priority. You must also keep up to date with insurance payments, or the creditor may buy costly insurance for you at your expense that may give you less protection. In most states it is illegal not to have automobile liability coverage. If you can give up one or more of your cars, you will not only save on the payments but also on gasoline, repairs, insurance, and license fees.

5. *Child support.* Paying child support is absolutely essential. Not paying can land you in jail.

6. *Other secured loans.* Beyond your home and car, debts on furniture, boats, RVs, and expensive electronic gear are likely to be secured—that means the lender can repossess for nonpayment. You know a debt is secured if you signed a security agreement. If the property is something you cannot live without and you think the creditor will take it for non-payment, you need to keep that debt current. Otherwise, consider it nonessential.

7. *Unpaid taxes.* If the IRS is about to take your paycheck, bank account, house, or other property, you need to set up a repayment plan immediately. If the amount you owe is less than $10,000 and you've never defaulted on an agreement with the IRS, you have the automatic right to a monthly payment schedule to pay your taxes. Even if the amount you owe is more than $10,000 or you've defaulted in the past, the service might still be willing

to negotiate a payment plan if you can convince the agency that you'll stick with it this time.

Nonessential Debts

These are financial obligations that will have a lesser and/or significantly delayed effect if you withhold payment for a limited time. Understand that to do so may cause blemishes to your credit file. But in the big picture a blemished credit report is easier to live with than being thrown out of your home or having your car repossessed.

8. *Student loans*. Most delinquent student loans are backed by the US government and the law provides for special collection remedies. These could include seizure of your tax refunds and special wage garnishment.

9. *Credit, department store, and gasoline cards*. The consequences for falling behind with these debts will be losing your credit privileges and, if the debt is unusually high, you may be sued.

10. *Loans from friends and relatives*. You should feel a moral obligation to pay, but these creditors will likely be the most understanding of your situation. Have an honest talk, explain your situation and plan, and then confirm your commitment to full repayment.

11. *Medical, legal, and accounting bills*. While these debts are real and will be paid eventually, they are rarely essential with one exception: if you are still receiving necessary treatment from the provider to whom you

owe money, you must keep up with minimum payments to prevent these services from being cut off.

12. *Other unsecured loans.* Every other debt you owe is probably in this category. These unsecured debts are rarely, if ever, essential to pay first.

Your role is to be a good steward and caretaker of the funds that flow into your life—meager as they may appear to be right now. Don't allow your emotions to dictate how you distribute them. Do not let your creditors set the agenda, either.

You must lead with strength, courage, and confidence based on good, sound principles. Do not hide, do not lie. Above all, do not take your situation personally. Adopt a businesslike mind-set and treat your creditors as you would want to be treated if the tables were turned.

Be courteous and respectful yet assertive. Do not make promises you cannot keep. And when your situation turns around (it will), keep the promises you have made to your creditors, your family, and to yourself.

15 An Invitation to Join Our Debt-Free Movement

> Debt-proof living is a way of life—a financially disciplined lifestyle that produces peace and joy. Debt-proof living is your invitation to a rich and abundant life.
>
> —Mary Hunt

I am asking you to make a decision right now that you will take the 7 Rules and use them to build a strong financial foundation into which you will drill deeply and drop the pilings of your life.

Learn the 7 Rules so well you can repeat them in your sleep. Hang on to them for dear life when your emotions go wild, when temptations overwhelm. Depend on them when everything in you wants to quit and go to that place that exists only in your imagination—where money is no object and you can spend with reckless abandon.

I can promise the foundation built on the 7 Rules will stand up under all kinds of circumstances. When the challenges come—and they will—your foundation will hold and you will come through strong.

I don't want you to make this journey alone. To do that will be unnecessarily difficult. Harold and I did it alone, so I know what of I speak.

A much better idea is to take the trip with others who are making the same journey, some who've been at it for a while and want to share their experience, strength, and hope. I have an idea for how you can find that kind of community, with an invitation for you to join us. But first, I want to pick up my story where I left off in chapter 2.

The Rest of My Story

In 1992, following a full decade of paying down our debt, experiencing the joys of living below our means, and starting our own industrial real estate company—I was becoming increasingly anxious to get the debt paid in full so we could just forget it ever happened and go on with our lives. Harold and I had paid off more than $88,000 of toxic debt but $12,000 still remained, and I was losing patience.

I needed to find a way to raise that $12,000 fast. I wanted to get it over and done with. I was bent on finding a way to earn extra income through some kind of side job or endeavor. That's when I got a wild idea to write a subscription newsletter, an idea that still makes me laugh. I'd never written anything but a real estate contract in my life! I was a trained musician, not a journalist. But still, the idea was there, and in my mind it held the promise I was looking for: the additional income we needed to rid ourselves of toxic debt.

My idea was to find 1,000 people to pay $12 to subscribe to my monthly newsletter, which would be on the topic of how to get out of debt and learn to live below your means—for one year. Sounded like $12,000 to me. That was the entirety of my business plan to found "Cheapskate Monthly."

Never underestimate the value of a simple idea when exposed to God's supernatural power. I know that idea didn't originate with me. I believe I was divinely led to step out and do something this bold, if not a bit odd by human standards.

I wrote the first issue, a copy of which ended up in the hands of a reporter for the *Los Angeles Times*. That led to an article, published above-the-fold on May 15, 1992. That article launched a fledgling newsletter into a national phenomenon. It hit the wire service, resulting in interview requests from every major newspaper in the US and media attention the likes of which I never dreamed.

Subscriptions started pouring in from every state in the union, and foreign countries as well. People were hungry to learn how to get out of debt and live below their means.

By all rights, I should have closed up shop at the end of that first year. But something happened that I'd not anticipated: I developed a passion for personal finance and teaching my readers all I could learn. I discovered I had a talent to write, speak, and motivate people to take control of their financial situations, pulling their financial futures from the stranglehold of the consumer credit industry.

I did raise the $12,000 we needed, and we paid off that final toxic debt. And I hardly noticed because my new position as editor of a national newsletter was in full bloom.

Shortly after the article ran in the *LA Times*, I received an offer to write a book (usually it goes the other way, that a writer proposes to a publisher to write a book), then another and another. With each issue of the newsletter and interview request, more and more people joined our debt-free movement, and my mailbox filled to overflowing.

Soon I began hearing from my readers how they were getting out of debt by applying the principles and following the steps they were learning. The stories were so empowering and encouraging, they were like rocket boosters to keep me reaching out to help more people struggling with their financial issues.

In 1996 we secured our first website URL, and "Cheapskate Monthly" ventured into cyberspace under the corporate umbrella Debt-Proof Living. Several years later, I wrote another book, *Debt-Proof Living,* that has become the text for the money management method by the same name. Sure, I told my readers, it's fabulous to cut expenses so we can live on the incomes we earn (I still have fun calling myself a "cheapskate"), but there is a bigger picture. We do this so that we can stop depending on credit to bail us out every time any little thing goes wrong or we face an unexpected expense. Debt-proofing our lives is about becoming financially responsible and not dependent on others to fund our lives—and to reach a point of financial independence.

DebtProofLiving.com has become an online community of untold thousands of people who are on the same journey to financial freedom. Some of the site is open to the public; however, members pay an annual fee to have full access to all of the member benefits, which include our exclusive online software for managing members' Freedom Accounts (Rule 4 reserves). The member forums are where DPLers come daily to find strength and support for the journey.

DebtProofLiving.com is a massive website, with a library filled with the hundreds of newsletter back issues; thousands of handy tips for how to save money on just about everything you can possibly imagine; member forums; unique calculators; our exclusive online software; and so much more. It has become a sizable community of like-minded people, all of us making the same journey to solvency and financial freedom.

Debt-proof living is not a righteous call to deprivation. It is not defined by austerity, poverty, guilt, and fear. It is not about extremes, bizarre behavior, misery, hoarding, or finding ways to recycle dryer lint.

Debt-proof living is a lifestyle where you spend less than you earn; you give, save, and invest confidently and consistently; your financial decisions are purposeful; you turn away from compulsive behavior; you shun unsecured debt; you borrow cautiously; you anticipate the unexpected; you scrutinize your purchases and you reach for your goals by following a specific plan.

Debt-proof living is about generosity, gratitude, and obedience. It is about sound choices and effective decisions. To debt-proof your life means knowing exactly what to do with your money and having the freedom to earn and spend it when and how you choose.

Debt-proof living is a way of life—a financially disciplined lifestyle that produces peace and joy. Debt-proof living is your invitation to a rich and abundant life.

Please consider this my personal invitation for you to join us at DebtProofLiving.com. Come and visit at your earliest opportunity. Grab some coffee, because you might want to stay for a while. It's a huge site. As a visitor you will have limited access; as a member you will have full use and access to the entire site. See page 203 for a special offer for *7 Rules* readers only.

I can't wait to welcome you into my DPL Family!

People Are Talking

"As a DPL member, I've become a wise consumer, and I continue to pay down my debt and fund my Freedom Account. Last Christmas I even paid for everything in CASH! First time ever." Connie

"First of all let me thank you for the opportunity to join your DPL family. These are the tools I needed to take control and put my finances in order. I'm just so excited and thrilled to have the tools to become financially responsible for the first time in my life." Sue, England

"I was thrilled to read your tips and tricks for how to pay down the principal on consumer loans quickly. I paid off a car loan in half the time doing that. My dad paid off his house in seven years! We saved so much in interest. Thanks for all your tips." Roseann

"Mary, I searched high and low all over the internet and could not find a Rapid Debt-Repayment Calculator as good as yours—not to mention all the wonderful articles and inspiration that we can have with you. Thanks." Suzie V.

"Because of you, in the last 18 months my husband and I have paid off approximately $10,000 of unsecured debt. The feeling of freedom is indescribable! In one week we will be closing on a new home. If it were not for your advice and encouragement, we never would have made it. We have learned so much. Thank you!" Nicole

"Initially I left my very large student loan off my Rapid Debt-Repayment Plan (RDRP), thinking it would only depress me. However, the way it works I will pay off all debt, including the student loan, much faster than I ever would have thought. I'm excited now to find areas of spending that were careless and apply those funds to my RDRP." Ralph

"I felt at ease after reading Mary's story and finding the DPL Community Forums. I read for about 48 hours straight, nonstop! I have visited the Debt-Proof Living Forum every day since I first signed up, and I've gotten incredibly valuable information from regular posters who are in similar situations." Ruby

"It is amazing how so many people you've never met or may never meet face to face can care so much about you and you about them. This has got to be the best group of people out there and I am thankful I found this place." Debbie

"Thank you for your books, this newsletter, and all your advice. Five years ago we had a lot of credit card debt and a pretty bad credit score. Now we are well on our way to being able to pay cash for our retirement home someday, hopefully someplace warm. Again, thank you from the bottom of my heart." Patricia

"I began reading this newsletter about six years ago and began working on my debt and improving my credit score. Since that time I've paid off $30,000 of debt, have more money in savings than I've ever had in my life, and my credit score is 881, which is higher than 90 percent of the population. Mary gave me the steps for success and much-needed encouragement along the way. Thank you." Pamela

"In 2005, I discovered Mary Hunt and read her book *Debt-Proof Living*. In it, Mary explains the value of giving and saving and how important it is to do this even when you carry debt.

187

"At that time, my life was debt-ridden, chaotic, and not going well, so I began applying Mary's 10-10-80 formula.

"As a member of Debt-Proof Living online, once a week I posted my spending in the Community Forums area under "Live the Plan." I still do that because it keeps me accountable.

"This DPL journey is continually unfolding. I read about the DPL Decade of Decision and my goal is to fully fund my Contingency Fund.

"I completed paying off my debts in 2008. I may not know what bumps or curves lay in the road ahead, but I do know that I have a valuable resource that I can rely on: Debt-Proof Living online.

"Thank you, Mary Hunt and DPL Central. So many minds working together. It's a beautiful thing!" Stephen

"In November of 2002 my husband was let go from his ministry position due to financial difficulties within the church.

"Once the initial shock of our situation wore off, we sat down together and came up with our game plan. My husband and I have been following the principles of Debt-Proof Living for several years. We had our Freedom Account and a fully funded Contingency Fund.

"Thankfully, we believed that the principles of Debt-Proof Living would put us in the best possible position to go through such a situation, and when it happened we did not panic.

"Debt-proof living principles and Mary's monthly encouragement gave us the strength to keep from falling into despair. This has truly been our miracle year." Andrea

"I want to thank Mary for sharing her debt story. I almost missed marrying a wonderful man because I was financially irresponsible.

"Signing up for membership at Mary's DebtProofLiving. com was one of the best investments I have ever made toward my financial health and peace of mind.

"When I first read *Debt-Proof Living* I was so far in debt that I was told by my fiancé that if I didn't do something about my finances I was going to lose the house I was buying.

I didn't even have enough money for groceries, so I would buy food with a credit card.

"I am grateful that Mary was humble enough to admit how bad her financial situation was because it showed me how to use the tools to become debt free. It just feels better to pay off what I owe than to claim bankruptcy." Theresa

"One day I sat and added up every bill I had—everything from student loans to car loans and everything between. The final number was over $35,000.

"I sought advice and read some books. Some of it was good, but most of it was really bad. One of today's top financial gurus suggested using my credit card to buy groceries! It sounded wrong so I returned the book and looked around some more.

"I found myself on Mary Hunt's website. Many of the other books made me feel hurt, embarrassed, and ashamed that I'd gotten into this place. Mary was like a warm hug. I destroyed $35,000 of debt in just four years.

"The principles of DPL still work even if you're not drowning in debt!" E.J.

Epilogue

It's Only Too Late If You Don't Start Today

In the mountain community of Running Springs, located 6,000 feet above sea level in the heart of the San Bernardino Mountains of Southern California, sits a small stone church that would be impossible to find if you did not have good directions.

For three weeks each spring, two signs appear. One reads "Daffodil Garden, Park Here." The other points to a narrow path that leads through a cluster of huge evergreens and over a thick blanket of old pine needles.

As you turn the corner it is impossible to remain silent as you get your first glimpse of the most glorious sight, something beyond imagination.

From the top of the mountain, sloping down over several acres across mounds and valleys, between the trees and bushes, following the slope of the land, are rivers of daffodils in radiant bloom. Everywhere you look the color of yellow blazes across the natural terrain as if God had just installed daffodil carpeting across the landscape.

As you try to wrap your mind around the fact that you're looking at five acres of flowers, you can't help but wonder aloud, "Who? How?"

It makes your head spin because the sight is so amazing, so unexpected and absolutely impossible. But there it is. You can see it, but you cannot believe it.

The Daffodil Garden is the handiwork of one woman. A former Los Angeles high school art teacher, she and her husband still live on the property. Their small home fits perfectly into the scene in the midst of all the glory.

This one woman, beginning in 1958, planted each daffodil bulb by hand, one at a time. No shortcuts. Year after year, planting just one ugly, dried up, lifeless bulb at a time, she forever changed her world by creating something of magnificence, beauty, and inspiration.

To date, she has planted by hand more than 1,000,000 bulbs. She takes it one day at a time, when the weather is good. Her goal is to plant 600 bulbs before lunch and 400 bulbs in the afternoon. She says that looking at 1,000 bulbs is just too overwhelming, so she breaks it up into manageable parts.

Each daffodil bulb produces from three to ten blooms. As you look around it's easy to believe that you are looking at 10,000,000 flowers, the golden expanse is that great.

Over the years, raging fires have destroyed this property not once but twice, taking with them the home and many of the trees. Each time this couple has rebuilt. But here is the most remarkable thing: the daffodils have always survived. In fact, some of the original bulbs from 1958 are still producing amazing blooms year after year, having never been watered or fed artificially. It seems that even when tried by fire, the daffodils hunker down into the safety of their deep roots, determined to survive. Every spring, they come back, more prolific and glorious than ever.

I don't know if the woman started with a 50-year master plan to cover a 5-acre hillside, but I doubt it. Instead, I'll bet she had a small goal to plant a patch close to the house. It looked so pretty, the next year she set a new goal for her daffodil patch to line the driveway. Then around the side of the big tree. Over the knoll, and along the mountain path. Just one small goal after another, year after year, she painted the landscape.

I can't help but think of you now as our time together is coming to a close and you set out to apply the 7 Rules to your life.

Whatever your goal, as you begin now to apply and live by the 7 Rules, don't think about how long the journey will be. Instead, set short goals.

You will be tempted to look backward. At times you will long to undo decisions you have come to regret, and you may be tempted to fall back into living with guilt and anxiety. That is a waste of time and energy and will only lead you to frustration. Don't wallow in the past. Instead, release your mistakes and go on.

Don't be hard on yourself by dwelling on what you could have accomplished if you had started years ago.

Instead of worrying that it's too late, think of what you will have missed if you don't start today.

Don't put this off until your debts are paid, the kids are grown, until you get out of school, until you find a better job, until you clean your closets, until you get married, until spring break, until next year, or any other excuse you can think of.

Because you are human, you will make mistakes in the future. But your failures can be a source of blessing as they humble you and give you empathy for others whose needs are far greater than your own.

Determine to find contentment in what you have. Look for needs around you that you can fill with some of your wants. Thank God for all that you have.

As long as you are heading in the right direction, every step will count for good—even the baby steps. And when you fall on your face, just get up and keep going. And going. And don't ever give up.

Before you know it you'll be changing the landscape of your world.

Notes

Introduction

1. Clark Howard, *Clark Howard's Living Large in Lean Times* (New York: Penguin, 2011), xi.

Chapter 1: The Cost of Financial Ignorance

1. "What American Teens and Adults Know about Economics," 38.121.131.180 /WhatAmericansKnowAboutEconomics_042605-3, pdf accessed 7-16-2011.

2. "Greater Fools," www.newyorker.com/talk/financial/2010/07/05/100705ta _talk_surowiecki, accessed 7-16-2011.

3. "The Financial Literacy of Young American Adults," www.jumpstart.org /assets/files/2008SurveyBook.pdf, accessed 7-16-2011.

4. "Financial Literacy and Ignorance," www.annalusardi.blogspot.com/2009/06 /protecting-consumers-regulation-is-not.html, accessed 7-16-2011.

5. Mortimer Zuckerman, "Housing Crisis Represents the Greatest Threat to the Recovery," *U.S. News & World Report*, posted Jan. 27, 2011, www.usnews.com /opinion/mzuckerman/articles/2011/01/27/housing-crisis-represents-the-greatest -threat-to-the-recovery, accessed 7-16-2011.

6. Kristopher Gerardi, Lorenz Goette, and Stephan Meier, "Financial Literacy and Subprime Mortgage Delinquency: Evidence from a Survey Matched to Administrative Data," Federal Reserve Bank of Atlanta, April 2010, www.frbatlanta .org/documents/pubs/wp/wp1010.pdf.

7. www.careerbuilder.com/share/aboutus/pressreleasesdetail.aspx?id=pr584& sd=9/1/2010&ed=09/01/2010, accessed 7-16-2011.

8. www.creditcards.com/credit-card-news/federal-reserve-g19-consumer-credit -march-10-1276.php, accessed 7-16-2011.

9. www.indexcreditcards.com/credit-card-rates-monitor, accessed 7-16-2011.

10. www.ftc.gov/be/seminardocs/100415debtliteracy.pdf, accessed 7-16-2011.

11. "Student Loan Debt Exceeds Credit Card Debt in the USA," www.usa today.com/money/perfi/college/2010-09-10-student-loan-debt_N.htm, accessed 7-16-2011.

12. "43% Have Less Than $10k for Retirement," money.cnn.com/2010/03/09 /pf/retirement_confidence/index.htm, 7-16-2011.

13. www.census.gov/prod/2009pubs/acsbr08-2, accessed 7-16-2011.

Chapter 2: My Story

1. Check kiting is the illegal act of taking advantage of the float to make use of nonexistent funds in a checking or other bank account.

Chapter 4: Rule 1

1. "Living Large: Home Size Increasing," www.wral.com/news/local/story /2443194, accessed 7-26-2011.

2. "Study: Average Size of New Home," www.cepro.com/article/study_average _size_of_new_home_drops_9_in_q3_2008.

3. "Electronic Amenities Top Homebuyers' Wish Lists," www.cepro.com/article /electronic_amenities_top_homebuyers_wish_lists_nahb_finds.

4. www.selfstorage.org/ssa/Content/NavigationMenu/AboutSSA/FactSheet /default.htm.

5. "Anywhere the Eye Can See, It's Likely to See an Ad," www.nytimes.com /2007/01/15/business/media/15everywhere.html, accessed 4-12-2011.

Chapter 6: Rule 3

1. See 1 Timothy 6:5–10.

2. See Deuteronomy 14:23; Exodus 36:5–7; 1 Chronicles 29:14, 16–18; Malachi 3:10; Philippians 4:19.

Chapter 8: Rule 5

1. www.bankrate.com/calculators/smart-spending/home-budget-plan-calcu lator.aspx.

2. Debtproofliving.mvelopes.com.

3. www.mint.com.

4. www.familyfn.com/kits/budget_kit.

Chapter 9: Rule 6

1. www.daveramsey.com/article/the-truth-about-your-credit-score/lifeand money_creditcards.

2. www.myfico.com/CreditEducation/WhatsInYourScore.aspx, accessed 7-2 -2011.

3. money.msn.com/credit-rating/lifetime-cost-of-bad-credit-201712-dollars -weston.aspx, accessed 4-30-11.

4. www.myfico.com/helpcenter/autos/get_better_rate.aspx.

Chapter 10: Rule 7

1. money.usnews.com/money/blogs/the-best-life/2010/12/14/baby-boomers-to-inherit-up-to-116-trillion.
2. www2.tbo.com/business/business/2011/jun/01/SPBIZO1-home-price-index-at-lowest-point-since-200-ar-234029.
3. newsfeed.time.com/2011/05/10/survey-85-of-new-college-grads-moving-back-in-with-mom-and-dad.
4. Proverbs 1:13–15; 17:18; 22:26–27; 27:13.
5. Proverbs 6:1–5.
6. Psalm 37:21.
7. Proverbs 22:7.
8. Deuteronomy 28:12.

Chapter 11: Getting It All Together

1. www.dominican.edu/dominicannews/study-backs-up-strategies-for-achieving-goals.html.

Index

Mary Hunt, award-winning and bestselling author, syndicated columnist, and sought-after motivational speaker, has created a global platform that is making strides to help men and women battle the epidemic impact of consumer debt. Mary is the founder of Debt-Proof Living, a highly regarded organization consisting of an interactive website, a monthly newsletter, a daily syndicated column, and hundreds of thousands of loyal followers. Since 1992, DPL has been dedicated to its mission to provide hope, help, and realistic solutions for individuals who are committed to financially responsible and debt-free living.

As a speaker, Mary travels extensively, addressing conferences, corporations, colleges, universities, and churches at home and abroad. A frequent guest on radio and television, she has appeared on dozens of television shows including *Dr. Phil*, *Good Morning America*, *The Oprah Winfrey Show*, and *Dateline*.

Mary lives with her husband in Orange County, California.

FREE Membership Offer *to*

Debt-Proof Living

As my way of thanking you for buying this book (and reading it . . . you read it, right?), I have a special offer for you to join Debt-Proof Living Online.

To take advantage of this offer, take your copy of *7 Money Rules for Life* and go to **www.DebtProofLiving. com/7MoneyRules**. Once there, you will find the location of a secret code, which is hidden within the pages of this book. I'll tell you exactly where it is. With that code you'll have all you need to redeem this offer. It's like a scavenger hunt! We're nothing if not a lot of fun at Debt-Proof Living!

Usually authors say good-bye to their readers when they come to the end of the book, but instead this could be just the beginning. I'm hoping the next time you hear from me I will be welcoming you to my Debt-Proof Living family!

Best,

Mary

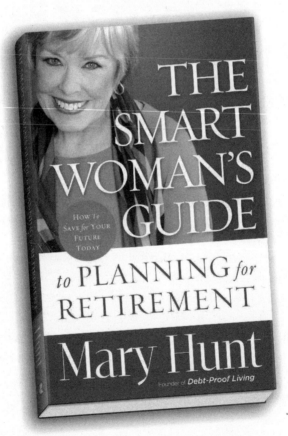

Want more debt-proof tips and tricks?

Explore DebtProofLiving.com/SmartWoman to find bonus material including:

- Slow cooker recipes

- New tools to help manage your finances

- Homemade laundry detergent recipe that fights stains and overspending

- Information about joining the new Retirement Forum

- And more!

"A great resource to have in your library."

—*Bookpage*

All the best advice you've ever heard (and plenty you've never heard) collected into one handy volume. Every tip is short, to the point, and helps you make the most of your money and your time, making everyday life less hectic and more enjoyable.

Debt-Proof
LIVING

Debt-Proof Living is a great big wonderful community offering help and hope to anyone who wants to learn how to manage their money more effectively. If you want to get out of debt—or stay out—and learn how to live below your means, Debt-Proof Living is the place to be.

Debt-proof living is a way of life where you spend less than you earn, you give and save consistently, your financial decisions are purposeful, and you work toward your goals by following a specific plan.

DebtProofLiving.com is the home of the debt-proof living philosophy. It is primarily a members-only website with features such as money management tools, articles, resources, community forums, consumer tips, recipes, and more. Here you'll find, in continuous publication since 1992, the DPL newsletter, which is published in an online format available to all members of this website.

Visit DebtProofLiving.com today to find out how you can debt-proof your life!

HILLSBORO PUBLIC LIBRARIES
Hillsboro, OR
Member of Washington County
COOPERATIVE LIBRARY SERVICES